BOSTON, 135 WASHINGTON STREET,
SEPTEMBER, 1852.

# NEW BOOKS AND NEW EDITIONS

PUBLISHED BY

# TICKNOR, REED, AND FIELDS.

## HENRY W. LONGFELLOW'S WRITINGS.

THE GOLDEN LEGEND. A Poem. Just published. Price $1.00.

POETICAL WORKS. This edition contains the six Volumes mentioned below. In two volumes. 16mo. Boards. $2.00.

In separate Volumes, each 75 cents.

VOICES OF THE NIGHT.
BALLADS AND OTHER POEMS.
SPANISH STUDENT; A PLAY IN THREE ACTS.
BELFRY OF BRUGES, AND OTHER POEMS.
EVANGELINE; A TALE OF ACADIE.
THE SEASIDE AND THE FIRESIDE.
THE WAIF. A Collection of Poems. Edited by Longfellow.
THE ESTRAY. A Collection of Poems. Edited by Longfellow.

MR. LONGFELLOW'S PROSE WORKS.

HYPERION. A ROMANCE. Price $1.00.

OUTRE-MER. A PILGRIMAGE. Price $1.00.

KAVANAGH. A TALE. Price 75 cents.

## NATHANIEL HAWTHORNE'S WRITINGS.

TWICE-TOLD TALES. Two Volumes. Price $1.50.

THE SCARLET LETTER. Price 75 cents.

THE HOUSE OF THE SEVEN GABLES. Price $1.00.

THE SNOW IMAGE, AND OTHER TWICE-TOLD TALES. Price 75 cents.

THE BLITHEDALE ROMANCE. Price 75 cents.

TRUE STORIES FROM HISTORY AND BIOGRAPHY. With four fine Engravings. Price 75 cents.

A WONDER BOOK FOR GIRLS AND BOYS. With seven fine Engravings. Price 75 cents.

## JOHN G. WHITTIER'S WRITINGS.

OLD PORTRAITS AND MOD. SKETCHES. Price 75 cents.

MARGARET SMITH'S JOURNAL. Price 75 cents.

SONGS OF LABOR, AND OTHER POEMS. Boards. 50 cts.

## OLIVER WENDELL HOLMES'S WRITINGS.

POETICAL WORKS. With fine Portrait. Boards. $1.00.

ASTRÆA. Fancy paper. Price 25 cents.

## ALFRED TENNYSON'S WRITINGS.

POETICAL WORKS. With Portrait. 2 vols. Boards. $1.50.

THE PRINCESS. Boards. Price 50 cents.

IN MEMORIAM. Cloth. Price 75 cents.

## THOMAS DE QUINCEY'S WRITINGS.

CONFESSIONS OF AN ENGLISH OPIUM-EATER, AND SUSPIRIA DE PROFUNDIS. With Portrait. Price 75 cents.

BIOGRAPHICAL ESSAYS. Price 75 cents.

MISCELLANEOUS ESSAYS. Price 75 cents.

THE CÆSARS. Price 75 cents.

LIFE AND MANNERS. Price 75 cents.

LITERARY REMINISCENCES. 2 Vols. Price $1.50.

## GRACE GREENWOOD'S WRITINGS.

GREENWOOD LEAVES. 1st & 2d Series. $1.25 each.

POETICAL WORKS. With fine Portrait. Price 75 cents.

HISTORY OF MY PETS. With six fine Engravings. Scarlet cloth. Price 50 cents.

RECOLLECTIONS OF MY CHILDHOOD. With six fine Engravings. Scarlet cloth. Price 50 cents.

## EDWIN P. WHIPPLE'S WRITINGS.

ESSAYS AND REVIEWS. 2 Vols. Price $2.00.

LECTURES ON SUBJECTS CONNECTED WITH LITERATURE AND LIFE. Price 63 cents.

WASHINGTON AND THE REVOLUTION. Price 20 cts.

## HENRY GILES'S WRITINGS.

LECTURES, ESSAYS, AND MISCELLANEOUS WRITINGS. 2 Vols. Price $1.50.

CHRISTIAN THOUGHT ON LIFE. Price 75 cents.

## WILLIAM MOTHERWELL'S WRITINGS.

POEMS, NARRATIVE AND LYRICAL. Boards. 75 cents.

POSTHUMOUS POEMS. Boards. Price 50 cents.

MINSTRELSY, ANC. AND MOD. 2 Vols. Boards. $1.50.

## JAMES RUSSELL LOWELL'S WRITINGS.

COMPLETE POETICAL WORKS. Revised, with Additions. In two volumes, 16mo. Boards. Price $1.50.

SIR LAUNFAL. New Edition. Price 25 cents.

## MISCELLANEOUS.

LYDIA: A WOMAN'S BOOK. By Mrs. NEWTON CROSLAND. 16mo. Paper, 50 cents. Cloth, 75 cents.

JOSEPH T. BUCKINGHAM'S PERSONAL MEMOIRS AND RECOLLECTIONS OF EDITORIAL LIFE. With Portrait. 2 vols. 16mo. Price $1.50.

VILLAGE LIFE IN EGYPT. By the Author of 'Adventures in the Lybian Desert.' 2 vols. 16mo.

PALISSY THE POTTER. By the Author of 'How to make Home Unhealthy.' 2 vols. 16mo.

WILLIAM MOUNTFORD. THORPE: A QUIET ENGLISH TOWN, AND HUMAN LIFE THEREIN. 16mo. Price $1.00.

JAMES FREEMAN CLARKE. ELEVEN WEEKS IN EUROPE, AND WHAT MAY BE SEEN IN THAT TIME. 16mo. Price $1.00.

CAPT. MAYNE REID. THE DESERT HOME, OR THE ADVENTURES OF A LOST FAMILY IN THE WILDERNESS. 12 Engravings. 16mo. Price $1.00.

WILLIAM WORDSWORTH'S BIOGRAPHY. By Dr. C. WORDSWORTH. 2 Vols. Price $2.50.

ROBERT BROWNING. POETICAL WORKS. 2 Vols. $2.00.

BARRY CORNWALL. ENGLISH SONGS AND OTHER SMALL POEMS. Enlarged Edition. $1.00.

RICHARD MONCKTON MILNES. POEMS OF MANY YEARS. Boards. Price 75 cents.

PHILIP JAMES BAILEY. THE ANGEL WORLD AND OTHER POEMS. Price 50 cents.

GOETHE'S WILHELM MEISTER. Translated by CARLYLE. 2 Vols. Price $2.50.

GOETHE'S FAUST. Price 75 cents.

CHARLES SPRAGUE. POETICAL AND PROSE WRITINGS. With fine Portrait. Boards. Price 75 cents.

CHARLES SUMNER. ORATIONS AND SPEECHES. 2 Vols. Price $2.50.

GEORGE S. HILLARD. THE DANGERS AND DUTIES OF THE MERCANTILE PROFESSION. Price 25 cents.

HORACE MANN. A FEW THOUGHTS FOR A YOUNG MAN. Price 25 cents.

F. W. P. GREENWOOD. SERMONS OF CONSOLATION. $1.00.

HENRY T. TUCKERMAN. POEMS. Cloth. Price 75 cents.

BAYARD TAYLOR. POEMS. Cloth. Price 63 cents.

R. H. STODDARD. POEMS. Cloth. Price 63 cents.

JOHN G. SAXE. POEMS. With Portrait. Boards, 63 cents. Cloth, 75 cents.

REJECTED ADDRESSES. By HORACE and JAMES SMITH. Boards, Price 50 cents. Cloth, 63 cents.

WARRENIANA. By the Authors of Rejected Addresses. Price 63 cents.

MEMORY AND HOPE. A BOOK OF POEMS, REFERRING TO CHILDHOOD. Cloth. Price $2.00.

ALDERBROOK. By FANNY FORESTER. 2 Vols. Price $1.75.

HEROINES OF THE MISSIONARY ENTERPRISE. 75 cts.

MEMOIR OF THE BUCKMINSTERS, FATHER AND SON. By Mrs. LEE. $1.25.

THE SOLITARY OF JUAN FERNANDEZ. By the Author of Picciola. Price 50 cents.

THE BOSTON BOOK. Price $1.25.

ANGEL-VOICES. Price 38 cents.

FLORENCE, AND OTHER TALES. By Mrs. LEE. 50 cts

SIR ROGER DE COVERLEY. Price 75 cents.

EACH OF THE ABOVE POEMS AND PROSE WRITINGS, MAY BE HAD IN VARIOUS STYLES OF HANDSOME BINDING.

# THORPE,

## A QUIET ENGLISH TOWN,

AND

# HUMAN LIFE THEREIN.

BY

WILLIAM MOUNTFORD.

BOSTON:
TICKNOR, REED, AND FIELDS.
M DCCC LII.

CAMBRIDGE: METCALF AND COMPANY.

# THORPE.

## I.

Quiet, ancient, and thriving is the look of Thorpe. It is a small place, and almost consists of one long street; at one end of which is a large square, with a market-cross in the middle of it, and with St. John's Church on one of its sides. At the other end of the long street is the Presbyterian Chapel, embowered in trees. There is a large graveyard round it. And on one side of the graveyard, in a garden, stands the Parsonage. In the long street, about the middle, are the almshouses for the widows of decayed tradesmen and farmers. They form three sides of a square, and are only one story in height. Agreeably to the will of the founder, and in accordance with what was the fashion three hundred years ago, the almswomen wear gowns of black cloth, and scarlet hats of a yard high, and a conical shape. And now and then one of them may be seen crossing the square, or coming out of the gate into the street, in her fantastic dress. In the long street there is many a half-timber house, with its high gable. And of the brick houses, a great number have their fronts all overgrown with ivy.

The surrounding country is a highly cultivated district; and all over it stand farm-houses, each one of them strong and cheerful. To nearly every house there is an open porch, with benches inside. In the yard, close by, stands a dove-cot; and a little apart, by themselves, are ranged the ricks of corn or hay, — two, five, ten, or even twenty.

On a fine evening in August, at Thorpe, two persons seated themselves on the steps of the market-cross. The one was about twenty-eight years of age, of a dark complexion, and bright, quick eyes. He was dressed in black, and looked languid. The other was a native of the village, but not a resident. And this one said, "Martin May, you are tired; so let us sit here a few minutes."

"What is the history of this town?" Martin May asked.

"It is very probable that of this place the beginning was this cross; and that the town grew up about it. Properly, Thorpe is an out-township of the last place we came through yesterday, before arriving at the Dell. And I suppose, in a gazetteer, you would hardly find this place mentioned under its own name. Nor would it be easy to decide what its name really is. For, like some other towns, it has several names, one of local and another of legal origin, and another perhaps derived from some forgotten circumstance. Now this place is called indifferently Thorpe, King's Thorpe, Thorpe Regis, and Crothorpe; which, no doubt, is a corruption of Cross Thorpe."

"A number of appellations! That is more curious than useful, I should think."

"But, May, about the character of the people there is no such dubiousness. You may believe what they tell you. And customs are none the less practices, and people are none the less trustworthy persons, for being in a town which calls itself Thorpe, but which the gazetteers and lawyers call by another name."

"And now tell me, West, as regards the inhabitants, what kind of a place is this?"

"O, that is for you to find out, now that I have settled you at the Dell, with my father, and shown you up and down the lanes, and seated you on the market-cross. O, my uncle Welby is coming this way. I will ask him your question. Uncle, what do you call this town as a place to live in?"

"Why, John, a sweet, beautiful spot! I have lived here fifty years and more; and it has always been the same; and it always will be as long as we deserve to have it so. It is we that ought to be better, not the place. Love, and union, and charity,—let us have that among us masters. Though, as it is, we are a good people here, a good, neighborly people. For there is not a man among us that means harm any way to any body, I think. And if there is, then I say see the country. See how the fields all lie laughing up at the sky; and how the lark soars up to sing under the sun; and how beautiful the little woods, the copses, are to look at, and how solemn to walk in! O, a sweet, beautiful country this is!"

When Farmer Welby had left, John West said, "That is just like my uncle. But see! yonder goes Miss Pinkey, with her nose up in the air. And she is of opinion that this is a dull town, an insufferable place: because there is not a theatre here, nor a fashionable church, nor any body, nor a monthly exhibition of the fashions. But here comes Abel Pratt. He is a laborer, with a large family and small means. Good evening, Abel. I am glad to see you looking so well. The times have been rather hard lately. Yet, on the whole, you think this town to live in is what one would wish?"

"It is a good, healthy place. As being God's it is very good, but not quite so good as being man's. That, I suppose, is the exact truth. Though some of the gentry are very well inclined to the poor at times, such as Christmas, or when there is the cholera. Yes, it is a very good place to live in, though rather hard for some of us sometimes. Now and then, towards the end of the week, I am very tired; and then the place does not seem to me so happy. But then directly there comes the Sabbath, and the minister's sermon. And so on Monday I am strong again for another week, and contented and happy. Good evening, gentlemen."

"Good evening, Abel."

"Who is this minister?" inquired Martin May.

"He is the Reverend Richard Baxter Lingard. And he will have to be your minister. For I suppose that on a Sunday your American Puritanism would scarcely be comfortable out of a meeting-house."

"But what is the meeting-house, the church?"

"It is called the Presbyterian Chapel. And it is my own place of worship."

"Your minister, then, is a Presbyterian. Is he very strict in his opinions?"

"For one opinion you would call him a Catholic, and for another a Unitarian; for one an Arminian, and for another a Quaker. But in reality he is a Christian; and it is all he wishes to be called. Though he says, if he must have a sectarian name, he would rather be called Presbyterian than any thing else, because it means nothing. Myself, I should call him an educated George Fox; and then, again, for some other reasons, I should not. For his doctrine he is answerable to no man, or synod, or bishop; not even to his congregation; but only to Jesus Christ and God. And this direct responsibility to the Head of the Church is our Presbyterian peculiarity. And for the maintenance of it, my ancestors were sufferers for many a year. And, indeed, one of them died in a prison, to which he had been sentenced by the bishop of this diocese, for refusing to attend service in that church opposite. I wish this evening Mr. Lingard would come this way, so that you might hear him talk. Ah, what does this village look like in his eyes, that are the eyes of the Spirit! That is what I should like to hear him say."

"What a rate that carriage drives at! It is a fine pair of horses. But what an odd livery the coachman wears!"

"It is Mr. Burleigh's. The Justice he is called here. And he now,—he thinks it is well there should be a place like this to send to for groceries or a surgeon. But otherwise he is of opinion that this town is a nuisance, as all towns are, except the county town and London,—mere harbors for insolence, and poachers, and radicals! Ah, here are two other witnesses coming towards us. One of them, the man in gray, is from the poor-house. And I suppose the other is somebody in his charge. So, Thomas, you are out of the house on leave this evening. How is this place now to live in?"

"Well enough, if it were not for the Master, who is so strict, and the Guardians, who want us to die faster than we do. So Scowley says. Though they have not said any thing to me about it yet. And Scowley does not always tell the truth. However, I think myself, that, if we have to go to church on Good Friday, we ought to have tea and sugar allowed us, the same as on Christmas day. But we have not."

"Well, that is not fair. Who is this with you? O, you say his name is Potts. Well, Mr. Potts, what kind of a place do you find this town?"

"Ay, ah! A place, sir, is it? Ay, it is a place, I believe. So I have been told. A place!"

"There, that is all. Good evening! Poor fellows! O, there out at his gate comes Dr. Scoresby. But he is not coming this way. However, I know what is his opinion of the town. He thinks that this is a very respectable place; but that the people in it neither marry nor die, nor want children baptized, as frequently as they do in other parishes. You will soon get to know him. He is a kind man and rather wealthy. O, here is Nurse Privet. Well, Nurse, how do you do? And just now how do you find this place to live in?"

"Indeed, sir, it is a very hard place to live in, for a woman like me, who has got to get her living ——"

"By other people's dying."

"No, master John, I do not live that way, at least not altogether. For I nurse ladies as well as gentlemen."

"And babies too."

"Well, so I do. But would you believe it? Just now there is not any body in all the parish that is likely to want me. Every body is so well; unless it may be this gentleman here. Ah, I know by his cheek. I know the signs. Please, sir, if you should want ——"

"Stop, you harpy. You will frighten him, and have him drop. Hands off! Not a word! He is not going to die. He is not going to be ill. He is going to eat bacon and beef and be well. It is what he is come here for. And, Nurse, if you will go down to the Dell to-morrow, I think there will be something waiting for you. Good night! And now here is Captain Jex. A fine evening, Captain!"

"It might be, Mr. West, if it were not so cold and damp."

"I never come here, Captain, but I like this place more and more. It is so quiet and happy. Do not you think so?"

"It is well enough, considering that there are more women here than men, and considering that now the rector preaches twice a Sunday, instead of once."

"But, Captain, it is a good place to live in."

"For Christians, that want to work out their promotion; because Scoresby says, the more temptations we overcome, the higher up in heaven we shall go. Abundant temptations here! And some of them in Scoresby's cellar. But there will nobody ever be hurt with them."

"Well, what are the other temptations?"

"Everywhere for every body, to covetousness, and matrimony, and drunkenness."

"Captain, I know you never have thought much of this place. But you are a man of taste and observation; so, now, among the towns and villages you have seen, what place is there that you like best of all?"

"Well, then, Mr. West, there is one place that I know, and that I call decent. It is in Spain, close by Saragossa, on the Ebro. Ah, if I had stayed there I should have been made Alcalde of the town. I should have been a member of the Cortes. I am sure I should have been. They are a fine, sensible people there. I should like to tell you some time what I did at that village, when I was stationed there during the war, under Wellington. I will tell you the next time I see you. But I must go now. This wretched weather does not suit me. Good night!"

"And now, Martin May, if you think that any night of his wishing can be good you are mistaken. A surly, conceited man! A sword always of bad metal, and now gone rusty! Does not he seem to draw the dark after him as he walks away?"

"Who, what? The old sword? But, West, why do you call these steps the Cross?"

"Because on the top here the pillar is part of what was a cross. The arms of the cross were broken off, I suppose, at the Reformation. It was erected here, some five or six hundred years ago, to commemorate some event, — something of struggle that ended in victory or resignation, when Edward the First was king."

While these young men were talking on the steps of the cross, the sun had set. And over all things it was twilight, deepening and deepening every minute, and reaching in through every window, and into every recess, as well as wide over the fields and into the woods. And like the twilight in an evening is Divine Providence. The Godhead spreads itself through human life, a silent influence on the souls of men, to inspire them with thought, or restrain them in power, or soothe them with peace; and it penetrates all actions, and makes them, each one, turn to what is divine, either in reward or punishment. And even as the deepening twilight reaches higher and higher up the skies, till at last the stars shine down it, so it is with the belief in Providence. And the more intensely it is seen to pervade the present with its power, the more certainly it is felt to connect us with the future by its purposes. Like the stars, they are visible only from afar, yet through Christ they are so distinctly plain,—the purposes of God toward us. And these,—how they enlighten, and draw, and sanctify us men, amid bewildered thoughts, in which we might be lost so easily,—and amid temptations, for which of themselves our own hearts would be too weak,—and amid that darkness of the grave, which sometimes clings about those who have wept for the dead too despondent tears.

## II

One evening there was a young girl called on Mrs. Satterthwaite, the housekeeper at the Parsonage, and sat with her in the kitchen. It was truly an English kitchen, — large, clean, comfortable, and queer. By the fireplace, and over it, there were old things of brass, copper, and steel, which never had been, and never would be, used. Mrs. Satterthwaite had polished them many years, and so had her mother before her. And her grandmother, who had first owned them, had always thought them much too good and new for use in her time. And now it had become doubtful for what purpose some of the articles had ever been meant. Against the wall stood a great, square piece of furniture, of black oak, full of drawers, and called a dresser. Over the dresser were a set of shelves, on which rested a few books, and three dozen pewter plates and dishes. The pewter was more than eighty years old; yet none of it had ever been used. The plates stood on their edges, and shone on the upper shelves. And on the lower shelves the books were laid. Among which were Pilgrim's Progress, George Herbert's Poems, Fuller's Holy War, Baxter's Saint's Rest, Fox's Book of Martyrs, Tusser's Hundred Points of Good Husbandry, and Quarles's Emblems.

"Well, Sarah," said Mrs. Satterthwaite, "I am sorry you are going, because I shall miss you in an evening some time; and I shall not see you at your mother's. But it will be all for your good, I am sure. I am glad of the good place you are going to. It will feel hard at first, — going from home. But do not think so, and then you will not find it so. To go to service is for a girl like going to college. It is the way to learn. And I have heard the minister say that in old times even lords used to be glad if other great lords would have their sons for waiters."

"I want to see and learn more than I can at home, Mrs. Satterthwaite."

"Right, Sarah, and now is your time, as I have told you before. And girl, you will never command, if you do not first learn to serve. And you will never learn, without you have your betters to teach you. With a good mistress, in a year you will get good habits for life. It will be your making for ever, — a place at a good house. I do not mean at a large house, with fashionable people: but I mean at a house where there are good ways from morning to night, — where the mistress knows what good work is, and how to have it done, and knows how to speak to a servant and advise her and cheer her, — and where the master is a right-minded man, whom it is a pleasure to serve. For, Sarah, it is both pleasanter and easier to serve some strict masters, than it is some slovenly men, who are satisfied, perhaps, with any thing. The lightest work is not always the best service, nor the easiest; mind that. Hard work goes easier in one house than no work at all does in another. But see here. I have got something for you. It is a present from the minister."

"O, how obliged to him I am! Such a beautiful box! And it is full of things, — scissors, bodkins, pins, needles. And, O, what a curious thing this is! O, how very much obliged I am! I am sure, I do not know how to thank the minister as I ought."

"Well, well, Sarah, I will tell him how you feel. Mind and make a good use of the box. And always, when you look at it, remember this, —

a stitch in time saves nine. Perhaps a less box would have been handier for you. But that did not occur to the minister, I dare say. For, as the proverb says, the greatest clerks are not always the wisest men,—not in every thing, at least. As how should they be? You will write soon, Sarah, and let us know how you are."

"O, yes, ma'am! I shall write the very day after I get to London. And very often I shall write. For I shall want to say so much of the new things I shall see, the fresh ways and people. It is said, there are such sights to see. Such shops and churches, and such crowds in the streets! But I shall often want to be out of it all and be at home."

"And as long as you want that, it will be all right with you. But perhaps you will not always feel as though home were the only thing you wanted. You will see bonnets and gowns, and shawls and ribbons and rings, that you will like, and you will see places you may like to go to, and companions you may like to go with, and new ways you may like to take to. But have a care. Things will all be so strange to you, that you will think and feel nothing right, at first. And so for a while beware of doing any thing at all but your plain duty. Believe yourself foolish for the first six months, and you will easily be wise afterwards."

Here Mrs. Satterthwaite paused, and then, looking intently before her, she continued, "Many go out for wool that come home shorn themselves. The road is well enough kept, that is rid of bad company. A wicked companion is an invitation to hell. Pride will have a fall. Buy one fine thing, and you must buy ten to look all of a piece. Better go to heaven in rags than to hell with ornaments. Out of debt, out of danger. All is fine that is fit. Now, Sarah, you will remember."

"Yes, ma'am."

"And do not be afraid of work. Feather by feather the goose is picked. Every thing has got to be done by somebody. I mistress, and you miss, who is to sweep the house? Think how well you can do your work, and not how easily. She that will thrive must rise at five; remember that; she that hath thriven may lie till seven. On with your work early, so that your mistress may come down and begin hers without waiting. What, keep a dog and bark myself! Never let your mistress have to say that."

"No, ma'am."

"More nice than wise; never be that. No

sweet without sweat, without pains no gains, — mind that."

"Yes, ma'am."

"Take care of your money. A penny saved is twopence got. A pin a day is a groat a year. Mind your temper. The least said, the soonest mended. Virtue itself without good manners is laughed at. An ounce of discretion is worth a pound of wit. An ant may work his heart out, and never make honey. You may even say your prayers out of time, and there is reason in roasting of eggs."

"Yes, ma'am, Mrs. Satterthwaite."

"Take care of your character. For it will not take care of itself, if it is ever so good. Indeed, the better it is, the more care it will need. Dirt is dirtiest on clean white linen. Make yourself all honey, and the flies will eat you up. Forewarned, forearmed."

"Yes, ma'am."

"Tell me, Sarah, is there any news at your end of the town?"

"Yesterday, Mr. Coke came to Mrs. Gentle's again. And Jane Bates says the gentleman could hardly get out of the carriage into the house, he is so ill. And there is an American come to the Dell to stay. He is quite a gentleman, though they say he has lived in the same town with black men, and been like a gipsy along with wild Indians in the woods. But you would not think so, to see him. They say he is very clever, and knows about every thing. And well he may; for he asks about every thing from every body, no matter who. One day, he talked an hour with a scissors-grinder, out in the open road, and then asked him how much he charged an hour for talking, and so gave him a shilling."

"Quite the gentleman, is he? Then I saw him at chapel, last Sunday afternoon, up stairs, in a corner of the gallery."

"Yes, ma'am, and he is so clever. He has been learning all about the old church, and been reading in the register along with the clerk for hours together. And he told Squire Horrocks the name of his great-grandfather, which the Squire said he had never heard himself. And he told, besides, what ought to be the name on that fine marble monument in the church, that is broken at the top; and which the clerk said nobody ever had told before that he had ever known of."

"What is he going to do here; do you know?"

"People say that Dr. Blinkhorn thinks he may be going to write a book. But Bessie, at the Dell, says he is come here for the country air to do him good; because all the Americans belonged here once. And she says the doctor has told him that he will die, if he does not give over talking so much. And so now he is not to speak to hardly any body, all the summer."

"And now, Sarah, do not you forget what I have been saying. Ah, well! we may give good advice, but we cannot give conduct. But God will, if you ask him. I wish it was not London you are going to. However, a good mistress is a good place. And the city is well enough, if you have a place in it that is good. Do not forget your prayers, morning and night. Begin the day with God, and you will begin it well. Every night, pray over all your actions of the day. Pray God to bless whatever you have done right, and to mend yourself and what you have done wrong. Open all your thoughts to him, if possible more even than you would to your mother, and ask him to pardon and pity and mend and sanctify you. And he will. I shall often think of you, Sarah. There, now do not cry. And you will remember what I have said; will you?"

"Yes, I will. You are very good to me, Mrs. Satterthwaite, very kind."

"And so will every body be, every body that

is good. And from nobody else do you want a favor. For the Bible says very truly, that the tender mercies of the wicked are cruel. I am told that London is a very wicked city. And so it must be, because it is such a large place. Look where you will, there is sin for your eyes to fix on. There is a temptation to extravagance in every shop-window, the milliner's, the draper's, the jeweller's. Speak who will to you, it may be somebody that means you harm. And you may lay hold of a new companion's arm, only to be led straight into a pitfall. Traps and pitfalls everywhere about!"

Sarah turned pale, clasped her hands, and cried, "O, how am I to know them? O Mrs. Satterthwaite, why did not you tell me of this before? I must not go. I cannot go. Indeed I cannot. I will tell my father that I cannot, I must not——"

"Sarah, you do not want to know any thing more than you do. A girl like you may walk to the end of the world, and never know harm or know of it. Now do not be flattered at that; or if you are, you are not the girl I think. For I do not mean that of yourself you are safe; but what I mean is, that the grace of God is safety for you to walk in. And I think you have it. But do not be too sure of it, yourself, or that instant you will lose it."

"You think, then, I may go? I am afraid, if I do, I may be tempting Providence. I am but a poor, foolish creature very often. And I am young and inexperienced, you know."

"Well, so you are. But whether you see danger or not will never matter. For you will never be in it, if only you keep looking at God. Walk with God; and bad persons will not speak to you, and indeed will hardly wish to. For there is a kind of innocence that is like a robe of protection; and you may walk in it, on the way of duty, and always be safe,—through traitors, and never know of them,—past pitfalls, and never see them,—through the fires of Baal, and never feel them,—and past the place where pleasure sits and sings, and never hear her, to mind her. Only, Sarah, keep your heart right with God, and then of themselves all things will be right with you."

"I am very much obliged to you for advising me; and I am sure, ma'am, I hope——"

Here Mrs. Satterthwaite extended her forefinger and said, "Good words cost nothing, but they are worth much. It is said, an idle brain is the Devil's workshop. So always have something good to think of,—a text, a hymn, or something you have learned at school here. And then away goes the Devil, when he finds the door shut."

"Yes ma'am."

"Put your finger in the fire, and say it was your fortune; never do that. Pray never to be led into temptation, and then walk into it of yourself; do not do that. You gazed at the moon, and fell in the gutter; never let that be said of you."

Here Mrs. Satterthwaite's tone changed from the authoritative to the womanly, and she said, "You are leaving a happy home, Sarah, a good father and a dear mother, and a place where you have had many, many joys. And you will often think of them. And because of your beginning life from a happy home, it will last you in courage for years. And wherever you are, I have no doubt you will seem to hear, often and often, the wind in the trees, and your father praying, and your mother reading, and the girls screaming merrily, as they come home from school. And with hearing the dear old sounds, you will be yourself, and keep so, I hope. Well, now, Sarah, good by. God bless you! And mind this, — to begin well is good, but to end well is better. Now do not look back. It is all nonsense, I know. But yet I shall throw the old shoe after you, for good luck. Good by."

## III.

During the time of the preceding conversation the minister was up stairs in his library, a long, low room full of books. He was a man of a mild, expressive countenance, lively manners, and musical voice. Notwithstanding his gentle look, and that peculiar air which grows upon a person from the silent company of books, there was in him great courage, decision, and energy, as he had several times shown upon public occasions. Like the four spirits, of whom Homer was one, and whom Dante saw, he was of semblance neither sorrowful nor glad. For nearly twenty years had he been a minister at Thorpe, and, like the Oxford clerk of whom Chaucer wrote,—

> "Sounding in moral virtue was his speech,
> And gladly would he learn, and gladly teach."

All day had he been reading and writing; and now, just as the sun was setting, he rose from his books, and went to a window. And as he stood at it, there came to him sounds from out of the town. And they occasioned in him thoughts perhaps of the loneliness of his own life, and perhaps of the evanescence of all life, and its being merely a sound, that dies with the making. And perhaps his thoughts were of his ever-varying success among his people, in his endeavor to walk among them, and guide them all aright. He sighed. And then he opened a volume, which lay upon a desk near the window. And half smiling, half sighing, he read from a discourse by Martin Luther: — "I myself do often feel the raging of the Devil within me. At times I believe; at times I believe not. At times I am merry; at times I am sad. Yet do I see that it happeneth not as the evil multitude wish, who would not give so much as a penny for preaching, baptism, and sacrament."

Then he returned to the window, and saw that the sun had gone quite down behind the window. And there came on the twilight of an August evening. And his soul grew calm with it; and it felt religious to him. And he said to himself, "Never, never do great thoughts come to a man while he is discontented or fretful. There must be quiet in the temple of his soul, before the windows of it will open for him to see out of them into the infinite. Quiet is what heavenly powers move in. It is in silence the stars move on; and it is in quiet our souls are visited from on high."

## IV.

The minister had been to Marley, and was returning home by the road across the meadows, and by the river-side. But he found Martin May fishing just at that point where the river makes a bend, and incloses the wood in the angle it makes. "Ah, Mr. May," said he, "are you a fisherman? I should hardly have thought you had been. You have come out for your supper, I suppose. Are you catching it?"

"Will you sit down, and rest yourself? Here, under this beech-tree, in this dry moss, and between these two roots, there is an arm-chair. As to my supper, I am very unlikely to catch it. Nor indeed is it what I have come for. Rod in hand, and with a basket, I have strolled by the water-side to this spot, thinking I might enter into the feelings of Isaac Walton, and perhaps have a talk with him in this sweet, quiet retreat."

"Ah, let me see! Yes, this is the book,—The Complete Angler, or the Contemplative Man's Recreation. Dear, dear old man! I could call him a saint. And if I do not, it is because I love him so much. A saint! No, he is not. He is not of the class of St. Benedict, who had the Devil come to him, in the shape of a little black-bird, and who then rolled himself in briers and nettles till he was covered with blood; nor of the class of St. Blaze, who scourged himself so thoroughly that seven holy women anointed themselves with his blood; nor of the class of St. Hilary, who obtained his wife's death by his prayers; nor of the class of St. Simeon, who eat only once a week, and even so was not wretched enough; nor of the class of St. Martin, who turned hermit, and lived on roots and wild herbs; nor of the class of St. David, who proved Pelagius to be an infernal monster by eloquence and miracles; nor of the class of St. William, who always wore a hair shirt, and never eat flesh-meat. No saint of any recognized class was Isaac Walton. But it may be said certainly that he was the most saintly of all who have taken the way to heaven, with the Bible in one hand, and a fishing-rod in the other."

"Was not there, sir, a St. Anthony who preached to the fishes?"

"Yes: and I have his sermon at home. The fish are addressed as dearly beloved fish. And at the end of the discourse they are said to have bowed to the saint, with profound humility, and a grave and religious countenance."

"Nor was Walton, with his hooks and flies, of the class of St. Anthony."

"St. Anthony never washed himself, and never changed his clothes. Two things were his especial abominations, cleanliness and Arianism. And very often it is said, that the Devil would haunt him and terrify him and confuse his intellects. More in the manner of Walton might have been Samuel Gardiner, who published a work on the Fishermen of Both Natures, Temporal and Spiritual, — a quaint, ingenious piece."

"Do you remember any thing of it, sir?"

"Only a little, Mr. May, and that not very correctly. Every fisherman has his baits, according to the fishes he angles for. For at a bare hook no fish will bite. And he who does not fish with a right bait shall never do any good. We that are spiritual fishermen have our different baits, suitable to the stomachs of those we angle for. And if we do not observe the characters of our auditors, and fit ourselves to them, we shall not do wisely. Let such as will not be led by love, be drawn by fear."

"Of what date is your quotation, sir?"

"It is of about the year sixteen hundred. The fisherman baits his hook, not only that the fish may take it, but be taken by it. The red-worm, the case-worm, the maggot-fly, and the small roach are glorious in outward appearance to the fish. And so the riches and the precedence of the world are but pleasant baits laid out for our destruction. The fisherman's bait is for a deadly deceit; so are all the pleasures of the world. As all the waters of the rivers run into the salt sea, so all worldly delights finish their course in the salt sea of sorrow."

"And so do most of our purer pleasures, too," said Martin May, with some sorrow in his tone.

"No; it is not so. We do not find it so, Mr. May. And therefore do not let us say we do. In our journey through life, we come upon a fountain of holy delight, and the stream from it we follow, day by day, and year after year. And perhaps then it vanishes, and leaves us to walk a dry and dusty and unlovely road. But that sweet stream, — is it lost in the salt sea of sorrow, along with the river of ambition and the muddy torrents of sensuality? O, no! It has not ended in the salt sea of sorrow, nor ever reached it. It has disappeared with perhaps the heat of the day in summer. And so not into the sea of hopeless sorrow, but into the sky it has gone. And if we are watchful, it will hold for us there the rainbow of heavenly promise."

There was a pause; for over the mind of Martin May these words had gone like spring-water, cooling, and refreshing, and brightening. And just now, from out of the depths of his memory, there were things glancing up at him that were lost indeed, but that looked up at him, beautiful and sweet, though very solemn.

The minister continued, "Worldly pleasures have in them nothing of immortality. And when they cease, earthly in themselves, they are altogether earthly to think of. And to remember, they are only memorials of the earth they belong to, and towards which they have been drawing us ourselves. But the sweet delights which God gives and which he takes away, — to look after them, we have to look up on high; and they draw up to them our hopes and faith. And though it be from far distances, yet smile upon us they do, — the forms of vanished good, and the dear, sweet faces we have known."

Again there was a space of silence, and then Martin May said, "That bird, that little brown bird, that is in and out of the hawthorn-bush so quick, — do you see it?"

"It is a wren."

"O, then it is the bird of which I overheard one child speaking to another, this morning: —

'The robin and the wren
Are God Almighty's cock and hen;
The martin and the swallow
Are God Almighty's bow and arrow.'

And the swallow is as swift as an arrow, almost. And sometimes the martin does bend his flight like a bow."

"Those lines," said the minister, "those lines were a part of my religion, when I was a boy, — and a very wholesome, useful, happy part. In winter, the robin is always about the house, and often close by the door. And I remember well the feelings I used to have for it of tenderness and awe."

"Is there any of that feeling now, do you think, among children?"

"O, certainly. In all this parish, probably there is not a boy, and I am very certain not a girl, who would hurt a robin or disturb its nest."

"Hush! what bird is that? It is like a cuckoo that stammers. A month ago, I saw a young cuckoo in the nest of a hedge-sparrow, and though only half-fledged, it was larger than the nest of its foster-parents. But there again! That hoarse stammering imitation,—can that be the cry of a cuckoo?"

"Yes, that is the way the bird ends the season. Though in the spring it comes with tones so clear and almost human.

'In April, the cuckoo shows his bill,
In May, he sings both night and day,
In June, he alters his tune,
In July, away he will fly,
In August, go he must.'"

"In April he comes, about what time?"

"In some parts of the country, the day after Swallow-day is known as Cuckoo-day. And Swallow-day is on the fifteenth of April. But the birds of passage do not arrive quite punctually, but a little earlier or later, according as the season is. But I believe that they come after one another in an order that is regular,—the swallow, and then the black-cap, and then the martin, and then the cuckoo, and then the fly-catcher. And fully a month later than the swallow comes the swift."

"The nightingale,—when does that come? But indeed I have never heard it yet,—not once."

"It comes in April, when it does come here; which it does not do always nor often.

'Sweet jug, jug, jug,
The nightingale doth sing
From morning until evening
As they are haymaking.'

That is a verse of an old ballad."

"And they leave at regular times, — these migratory birds?"

"Yes. And at regular times come their successors in their places, for the winter, — the woodcock, the snipe, the fieldfare, and many others, especially one on the eastern coast, a great gray bird, with black wings, called the Danish crow."

"Longest day, Shortest day, New Year's day, Midsummer day, Swallow day, Cuckoo day, — I like this naming of the days. I like to feel my life, as it goes forward, keeping time with the great harmonies of nature."

"And of God. This very month, among the ancient Rhodians, the children used to go from door to door swallow-singing. The first verse of the song was: —

'The swallow! The swallow is here,
With his back so black, and his belly so white;
He brings on the pride of the year,
With the gay months of love and the days of delight.'

Another custom among the Rhodians was that

of men who went about singing the song of the crow, and making a collection for him."

"Well, I am glad I had not caught a fish when you came."

"And myself," said the minister, "I had rather think of Isaac Walton as taking no more fish than his Kenna actually needed for the table. So long, long ago! And one can feel yet what kind of a woman Kenna was, and what her love for Isaac must have been. A quiet, affectionate, reflective woman, and not without energy at proper times, and one who raised her eyes, every now and then, to Isaac's honest face, with such admiration and loyalty. But oh! that song! What a gush of sweet sound! It is a thrush. There, on the bush across the water. A fine songster! Do not you think so?"

For a while Martin May did not answer; and then he repeated the following lines in a voice that trembled a little:—

"'There sat upon a linden-tree
  A bird, and sang its strain.
So sweet it sang, that, as I heard,
  My heart went back again.
It went to one remembered spot,
  It saw the rose-trees grow,
And thought again the thoughts of love,
  There cherished long ago.

"A thousand years to me it seems
 Since by my fair I sate,
Yet thus to have been a stranger long
 Was not my choice, but fate.
Since then I have not seen the flowers,
 Nor heard the birds' sweet song:
My joys have all too briefly past,
 My griefs been all too long."

And then, as if afraid of any remark, he added quickly, "What did you call that bird? How it does sing! What a song of exultation!"

"It is called the thrush, the missel-thrush, and sometimes the storm-cock, on account of its singing before and up to the coming of a storm. And this bird now must be singing against a storm. For see yonder sheep, — how they are all drawing together towards the corner of the meadow. Ah, yes! and this little flower, the pimpernel, — see, it is shut! O, it will be welcome, a little rain! Come, let us go. We shall just have time enough to reach shelter probably. For I am quite certain behind this wood there is a black cloud coming up. A cloud, Mr. May, that will rain for us, — no, not with our looking on; but which to-morrow will be known to have rained out of its black garb green grass, and flowers blue, white, yellow, red, and pink."

## V.

The next Sunday that Martin May attended chapel, after the conversation by the river-side, it seemed to him as though, by some agreement, the whole congregation had gone into mourning. Many of the men had scarfs on their shoulders, some of them of black silk, and some of them of crape. On his way to the chapel he had noticed that several men, besides having these scarfs, wore, tied round their hats, long, wide bands, which hung down their backs; and he had wondered at the meaning of these signs. Round the pulpit there was hung drapery of black cloth. And over all the crowded congregation there was an unusual stillness. The minister had on a scarf of black silk; and when he commenced the service it was in a voice of deep feeling. And then Martin May remembered to have heard during the week of the death of a lady, a young mother, who had been widely beloved in the neighborhood, and been very tenderly dear at home. He saw sitting in his pew the young man who was evidently the widower. And at the sight of him he wept helplessly; for there came over himself so wretchedly the sense of loneliness.

In his sermon the minister spoke of God and the earth, — how the earth may be our birthplace, but how heaven is our home, — and how from on high God reaches down among men to draw up to himself prayers, and love, and souls. He spoke of true affection as never ceasing, — elicited, perhaps, with a glance or a word, but outlasting the death of its object and the slow lapse of life. He said, it may perhaps be so, that we may outlive our friends a long time, and forget their words and looks, but still that there is with us the love they quickened in our hearts, and that it lasts on in us, life, happiness, and a purifying power. And he concluded with saying, "Sabbath by Sabbath, when we come into this place to worship, is not it over the graves of former generations? And the shadow of death upon us, — it is from beneath this that we enter into higher and yet higher worship. We disciples of the Man of Sorrows, — we believe this; — let us also come to the knowledge of the truth."

All this it was as though Martin May heard and yet did not hear. It went through his mind with a sweet, soothing effect, but was hardly any of it retained; and when he left the chapel, he felt as though he had been weeping all his old tears over again, only that they had been less bitter than before.

In the afternoon the minister discoursed from the same text as in the morning, but in a more general way. In the morning the sermon seemed to be directed to the pews in which the mourners sat; but in the afternoon the minister appeared to have in his eye the whole congregation. He began with saying, "This year it happened that St. David's fell upon a Sunday. But the sermon which I had prepared for that day I was prevented from preaching. Some portions of it I shall address to you this afternoon. And I can do so the more properly because St. David's, as a festival-day, commemorates not the royal Psalmist himself, but only his name, as borne by his namesake, an archbishop of Wales." This the minister said, partly in explanation of the nature of the sermon, and partly because he knew that there are some minds which are more effectually comforted by words not spoken with a view to themselves especially.

Of this sermon Martin May, on his return to the Dell, wrote out his recollections at length. For he said to himself, "I feel as though to-day were a crisis in my spiritual life; and I could wish to preserve some memorial of it." And so he wrote the following: —

"'Your heart shall live for ever.' — Ps. xxii. 26.

"So said David to his friends, in a time of distress. And at least his own heart is living still, and at this day is more widely felt than ever. The Psalms of David, — we read them for instruction, we sing them for joy, and we repeat them for sorrow and remorse; and not we only, but millions, and nations to the ends of the earth, — the child in his simplicity, and men and women in their experience, — the backwoodsman in the primeval forest, and the dweller among the tombs and the roofless ruins of ancient Rome.

"The heart of David! how it throbs among us, — making us feel, as David himself felt, — weep, as though with his wet cheeks to look at, — and rejoice, as though within hearing of his harp, — and mourn, as though in his sin we were reminded of our own, — and clasp our hands, as though with his helplessness, — and look up on high, as though emboldened with his confidence, — and pray, as though with his voice in our ears, trembling, and sobbing, and sublimely trustful.

"'Why art thou cast down, O my soul? and why art thou disquieted in me? Hope thou in God: for I shall yet praise him for the help of his countenance.' 'Create in me a clean heart, O God; and renew a right spirit within me. Cast me not away from thy presence: and take not thy Holy Spirit from me. The sacrifices of God are a broken spirit: a broken and a contrite heart, O God, thou wilt not despise.' 'Let the words of my mouth, and the meditation of my heart, be acceptable in thy sight, O Lord, my strength and my redeemer.' 'The Lord is my shepherd: I shall not want. He maketh me to lie down in green pastures: he leadeth me beside the still waters. He restoreth my soul: he leadeth me in the paths of righteousness for his name's sake. Yea, though I walk through the valley of the shadow of death, I will fear no evil; for thou art with me; thy rod and thy staff, they comfort me.' 'I have set the Lord always before me: because he is at my right hand, I shall not be moved. Therefore my heart is glad, and my glory rejoiceth: my flesh also shall rest in hope. For thou wilt not leave my soul in hell: neither wilt thou suffer thy Holy One to see corruption. Thou wilt show me the path of life: in thy presence is fulness of joy; at thy right hand there are pleasures for evermore.'

O the times these words have been said, and David's heart in them been felt throbbing and warm! O the people that have used them, — priests in the temple at Jerusalem, — captive Jews, by the river of Babylon, — the early Christians, in their secret worship, — sinners, trembling with God's angry eye upon them, — saints, feeling themselves all the more unworthy, the nigher a Holy God their lives advanced them, — righteous men, outcasts of the world, joying to feel themselves cast upon God, — good men, communing with God all the more earnestly for being lonely souls in a crowded earth, — men with such a yearning for God as only some prophet's words could speak, — sufferers, with a faith in them greater than their own utterance, a spirit bearing witness with their spirits, — dying men, praying their truest as well as their last, — widows and orphans, with only dead dust to look at for what had been their friend, but with an immortal soul to believe in, safe beyond corruption and the grave!

"And O what things the Psalms have outlasted, — the national existence of David's own people, — the destruction of Jerusalem, and the burning of the temple, — the rise and fall of kingdoms, — the prevalence of many a language, the Egyptian, the Chaldean, the Greek, the Roman, and the

Gothic, — the erection and the fall of great buildings, castles, churches, and cathedrals, — forgotten names, the world once echoed with, — the fame and dread of kings, — the foundation and the disappearance of cities, — and, one after another, a hundred generations of men, their lives and their exits by death.

"We may well believe they will last for ever, — the Psalms with David's heart in them; for they have outlasted so much already, — thirty centuries of time, myriads of books, and the laws and customs of a hundred nations.

"Ages hence, for the men of another era than ours, there may be other institutions than what we live under, — and other customs than what we use, — and clearer lights to walk by than shine on our prejudiced paths, — better ways of travel than we know of, — and larger comforts from nature than are obtainable yet, — and more justly famous names than we talk of. But in that future, far away among men, we do not know how to name, — in the great, dim future, that is to brighten, and open, and disclose such wonders, — there will be living still the heart of David, — living and to live for ever.

"And oh! with us, and in us ourselves, how it lives, — that heart of David's, — what comfort and encouragement and faith for us! O the desolate way the soul feels often, — so strange to God, as though unknown to him, — so cold towards God, as though warm with his love it never had been, or could be, — so worthless in itself, and unworthy God's notice, as though mind it, or love it, he did not and could not. With words of our own, any, the most earnest, we ourselves can pray; sometimes it feels as though God's ear we could not reach. But we say, 'Let the words of my mouth, and the meditation of my heart, be acceptable in thy sight, O Lord, my strength and my redeemer.' And by saying along with David, we feel along with him, and we thrill with the force of his holy words, and we feel them reach the listening ear of God. Another time we feel so depressed with recollections of folly and sin, that for prayer we have no heart, and we could wish to disappear from the sight of God for ever. But we have the words of another to pray with, — a transgressor's words. And with his repentant words we can speak, and weep, and repent, and pray, and be reconciled. 'Have mercy upon me, O God, according to thy loving kindness; according unto the multitude of thy tender mercies blot out my transgressions. Wash me thoroughly from my iniquity, and cleanse me from my sin. For I acknowledge my transgressions; and my sin is ever before me. Against thee, thee only, have I sinned, and done this evil in thy sight.' And with David's wording of it, sin itself feels like what draws God's eye in pity on us. Often it feels such a mere nothing as to be worthless almost, our human life. But we say along with the Psalmist, 'Behold, thou hast made my days as a handbreadth, and mine age is as nothing before thee.' And, overshadowed by God, our lives feel shorter still, but also strangely hopeful and trustful. And there are despondent seasons, when we feel so useless and worthless, that almost we could despair of the life to come. But with repeating David's words there quickens between us and God a feeling of alliance, — a bond to trust to, — a relationship stronger than death. 'I have set the Lord always before me: because he is at my right hand, I shall not be moved. Therefore my heart is glad, and my glory rejoiceth; my flesh also shall rest in hope. For thou wilt not leave my soul in hell: neither wilt thou suffer thy Holy One to see corruption.' O, how it lives on among us, — David's heart, — helping and blessing, inspiriting and inspiring us!

"And this life of his heart in this world, — is not it a sign, a token, some evidence of David's own, his soul's life with God? For it cannot have been extinguished for ever, — a heart so strong that its words are echoing about the world still, and as loud as ever. Thousands and tens of thousands, and millions and tens of millions of people turn their faces toward God, looking in the direction David showed. And himself he is where we look to; he is before the throne. We look in the direction of his words; and it is after his soul also. It must be; we feel it must.

"Age after age men worshipping in his spirit, and David himself perished! It cannot be. Everywhere now, and for three thousand years, men have been affected, as you and I are, with the feelings and the movements of David's heart. Its thoughts lasting on, thousands of years, — its devoutness still yearning, — its remorse still weeping and groaning among us, — its faith still living and earnest, — its hope and trust still making themselves felt among us; and the heart itself extinct! It cannot be. No, David, no, 'your heart shall live for ever.'

"And live it does, and helps our own belief in immortality. The heart of David, — it sustains our faith. For it throbs in our breasts, and thrills us with feelings by which we are sure of our being more than earthly, more than mortal. That great heart, — we receive it into our souls; and it is life in them, and strengthens them, and makes them feel earnest, — creatures of God, — and to live for ever.

"And yourselves, it is out of the heart that you best help one another, and that you most surely trust and feel yourselves immortal. And more than any thing else, either of your attainment or your nature, it will be 'your heart shall live for ever.'

"It is out of the heart that you help one another most effectively. You may be ever so learned in history or science, be ever so well acquainted with the ways of the world, and you may be ever so ready to impart your information; but you will not effect much good with your conversation, if you have not a good heart in you. For without that, you merely mortify people with your superior knowledge. And without it, also, logical power in any one exasperates, and wit provokes. Not the man who is all memory, and reasoning power, and science, and acuteness, — not he is of most good as a companion or a citizen; but he who is a man of heart as well as head, — a man of feelings, — a man of reverence, awe, fear, love, devotion, trust, and faith, — a man that feels himself circled about with infinity,—who is sensible of a million dangers about him, God's invisible shield keeps off,—who is tender with the feeling of his being mortal,—lowly, as though with his pride abashed by the watchful eye of God,—fearful of sin, as knowing of the secret ways it steals upon the soul,—who is affectionate in word, and look, and service, cheering men's souls with the very look of him, and strengthening for them unconsciously their belief in the goodness of the world,—a man that walks the earth in the faith of heaven, moving among things that are seen, mindful the while of things not seen and eternal, God's great purposes that compass him about even here, and that reach away into eternity. Such a person may be wanting in science, and be not very widely read in history, and not be very quick at an argument, and have no great wealth, with which to be generous. But he blesses men with what is better and rarer than money, and in ways in which the mere intellect is helpless. From the heart that is in him, such a man blesses with an everlasting blessing, even in chance words sometimes; and he carries about him, like an atmosphere, the presence of God, for men to feel; and he speaks in a manner that tunes men's minds to cheerfulness, and braces them to honesty. Yes, from the way you smile, the manner you speak of God, the tone of your voice, as well as from your actions and your serious words, it will be so, — it may be, and we will trust it will be, — that, by its effects on the minds of your children, acquaintances, and friends, 'your heart will live for ever.'

"It is out of the heart that we can best feel and trust our immortality. The heart is its own witness as to a life to come. It is consciously immortal. Not so the intellect. You may grow ever so learned, and scientific, and logical: but you will not therefore find yourselves grown more hopeful, more believing. No! The mere intellect testifies about itself almost only this, 'Vanity of vanities, all is vanity.' It is with the heart a man believes; with his feelings, and not at all without them; with love that cannot endure to be mortal, — with worship that feels itself coeternal with the God it yearns upon, — and with all those spiritual states that result from talking with God, and acting for him. Every day you may be strengthening in faith as to a hereafter; and you ought to be. For indeed every prayer you breathe that is earnest, every act of patience with pain, because of God, every instance of self-humiliation for sin, every sigh for your meanness before

God, every recollection of God as holy or watchful, and also every instance of interest in the moral welfare of another, whether a child or a man, and even every joy you have that is pure,—these all, things small and great, may help you to feel that 'your heart shall live for ever.'

"'Your heart will live for ever,' and more than any thing else, either of your nature or your attainment. O, how many a characteristic will fail us hereafter, and leave some of the first of us last! And how many a quality that is now little will hereafter be a qualification distinctive and great! It will fail the merchant, the forethought that is like the mastery of the market,—the quick discrimination, which sees great profits in small openings,—and that aptitude of his for business, which is all the more successful the more exactly it is business-like and nothing else. It will fail the artisan, that cunning hand that is now his pride and living. It will fail the good mother, the skill that keeps the house warm and clean,—the knowledge that keeps it tasteful at the smallest cost,—the ability that gathers into it comforts from markets, and shops, and gardens,—the orderly management that keeps regular the on-goings of the family, and the day and the week. It will fail him, the man of mind and philosophy, the learning of his books, the science of the universe. For it will be quenched, even his lamp of science, in the full blaze of the Godhead, the brightness of God's uplifted countenance. Of mere ingenuity, and learning, and ability, so much must fail us on the floor of heaven, — left behind with the world it knows of, and to perish with it.

"But it will live on and for ever, your heart, — your feelings of reverence, and obedience, and resignation towards God, — your feelings of mystery, and awe, and wonder about this universe you live in, — your faith in the future, as having in it more and more of God to show, — your patience, and commiseration, and love towards them that are of your household, and neighborhood, and town, and country.

"The beginnings of life immortal, — they are with you now. And it is for you to grow into them more and more. All life is overspread with the beginnings of the great, sweet, earnest hereafter. Grow into them, — patience with pain, because of God that allows it, — forbearance with a wrong-doer, because of the God that looks upon you both, — the feeling that draws husband and wife, and parents and children, to the utterance of a common prayer, — the motive on which, from the streets about, men meet at the house of God, —

the dear, thoughtful quiet of the Sabbath, — the sympathy that rejoices with them that do rejoice, and weeps with them that weep, — the welcome awe sometimes with which God flashes across our souls in the streets, or at our work, — the strange persuasion there sometimes rises in us of judgment to come, — what little meaning there is in saying, 'Good morning,' or 'Good night,' or 'Good by,' — the exaltation that ensues on dutiful effort, and the peace that follows prayer. Give into them, grow into them, for signs these are, and beginnings of the way 'your heart shall live for ever.'"

## VI.

The Past, the Past! There is no going back to it. There is a gate fast shut against us. And through that gate we can see and hear, but we cannot return. At that gate had Martin May sat mournfully for many months, looking back on scenes which day after day seemed farther off, and listening to kind voices. And among these voices was one so tender and solemn, that often, with hearing it, he would weep and bow his head upon his hands in anguish. But one day it seemed to him that this voice echoed some of the very words he had heard from the minister on the Sabbath: "Is it the highest love we feel, — love from the innermost sacred recesses of the heart, — when we grow weak with it and not strong?" And he said to himself, "I am wrong. I must change. I must be the better for the good which has been, and not the worse." But still the present was distasteful to him, and the future was repugnant to think of.

The Past, the Past! O, how it reaches after us, with a thousand hands, from Jerusalem and Rome, from old Saxon times, and from out of Norman castles, from out of ancient pulpits and tombs, and from every place wherever men have lived and died, — hands, many of them stretched after us to bless us, some of them by making above us the sign of the cross, and some of them by letting our fevered spirits feel the coolness of their touch, and some of them by pointing us to a walk in life, humble and quiet, and with God in sight.

The past, the past! O, how grateful to walk in are its long shadows, for a man who has been smitten by the heat of the noonday of life!

As a shadow from the heat, — it was for this reason that Martin May began to feel an interest in the antiquities of his neighborhood; though he himself thought he was fond of them for the sake merely of the exercise to which they drew him in walking and riding. And gradually, as his gloom passed away, he noticed, not without some astonishment, a new tendency in his mind to humor. Not that he had any pleasure in it, but that it was so he felt! And he thought he understood how it was, in other ages, that artists should have decorated churches with sculptured satires, and grotesque carvings; being themselves all the while men of earnestness and reverence and holiness.

He made journeys to ancient ruins, he sought out old relics, he became curious in the history of provincial words, he would sit and listen to rustic traditions, he felt an interest in the superstitions of the peasantry and their old customs. And for the time he agreed with Plautus, that they are wise who have a regard for ancient stories.

## VII.

One afternoon, half a mile down the street from the Parsonage, the minister went in at the gate of the garden before Mrs. Gentle's house. The house was low and wide, and all over the front was covered with ivy. It was the house at which lodged Mr. George Coke. The minister found Mr. Coke seated at the window, in an easy-chair. He was a man of forty-five years of age, and of a graceful, dignified appearance.

"Yes," said Mr. Coke, "I am ill. I am very ill. And I have come away from the noise and business of Manchester, to think awhile here and die. And it will all end in a handful of dust soon, all that I have been."

"But such dust as God watches,—dust such as angels may grow from, on the morning of the resurrection."

"What day of the month is this, Mr. Lingard?"

"It is the twenty-fourth, — St. Bartholemew's day."

"And so time goes! How it mocks us, does not it? Two months ago, and almost I was longing for this very day. It is come; and I did not know it was. I thought to have had it be a day of political success, joyous with twenty thousand voices of acclamation. And it proves to be a day in a sick room, a sick chair, and on sick diet."

"Yes, Mr. Coke, it is so life is."

"Or if the day does not alter from its expected character, then it deludes us in another way. It comes, and it comes: nearer and nearer it comes, and then it is gone. You cannot say of any moment that it is here, for even while you say so, and quicker than you can say, 'It is here,' it is gone. And a great day comes. It comes from out of infinity, and through a rainbow of promise: swift and joyful it comes. And then, before we have rightly felt it, it is gone past. A long-expected day, a day of fond wishes, and perhaps of earnest prayers, comes along nearer and nearer to us. It is like a beloved friend with its coming. And so we stretch out our arms to embrace it. But it slides past us. And we draw back our arms, and fold to our breasts nothing."

"But to our hearts we do fold experience."

"Yes, Mr. Lingard, and such experience as there is no gainsaying. We mortals, we are made to feel ourselves more and more mortal. O the years we look to in youth, so radiant and blissful, years of honor and success and love! They come; but they do not come as they looked. They go past us, but they do not feel what we hoped. And to look back on, they are all deceit; and they call to us, as though mocking us. It is for our good, I suppose. And it is to make us feel what weak, worthless creatures we are, amid the invisible things even of this world, and therefore how much more we must be so, as having among us the powers of the world to come."

"This nothingness," said the minister, "this nothingness, which life feels, is from the exercise of the hand or the intellect merely. The life of the heart, — that never feels illusive nor transient. The affections may have laid hold of the nearest objects and grown about them, and therefore may have clasped what was unsuitable, unworthy, or what may have died and fallen. But always the affections themselves feel real and eternal. Indeed, sir, I think you would say, from your own experience in the world, that the heart may be disappointed in one object and another and another, but yet still believes in some rest to be found, some ——"

"I think," said Mr. Coke, "you said that this was the twenty-fourth of August; did not you? Pardon my interrupting you. But it does seem to me so strange that this should be the day it is. Long as I have known of their having been open for me, — the gates of the City of the Dead, — yet little did I think, a month ago, that to-day I should be approached to within such near sight of them."

"And behind you, Mr. Coke, a life not without some useful actions done along its course."

"I think so; but, sir, I do not feel so. And this is so strange. Altogether worthless, and not worth remembering, feels now many an action of energy and integrity, and eminent success and public use. I find them no glory to look back on, — some few days of virtue, which I have formerly hoped might, to remember, be some comfort and spiritual assurance against death."

"Down in the valley of the shadow of death, the soul is so earnest, that of necessity all her previous experiences, the best of them, must be, to recollect, comparatively cold and mean."

"So strange it is, sir, so illusive! I suppose it is for the purpose of humbling us men, and making us feel that there is nothing of our own building that will last, — no foothold in life but will fail us, — no wise word but will sound like folly some time. And it is as though, for comfort or pleasant remembrance, there were no reliance to be placed on even such things of our doing as have in them the most of virtue."

"But," replied the minister, "rightly understood there is. For on the book of the Divine remembrance our virtuous actions are always the same that they ever were; and the record of them never fades. To our own feelings they alter in value, but not to our feelings as being illusive, but as having grown more earnest. The earnestness of philanthropic politics, and upright trade, may well feel to ourselves like nothing, at the end of life; the best earnestness of the world feeling quenched and worthless in the new earnestness of the world's end, and which is not without a something in it that is divine. But, as you say, it must indeed be strange to look back on life from under the shadow of death."

"See, sir, on the book-shelf yonder lies the newspaper. No doubt there is my name in it, in more places than one. But it has never been opened. And to me now all the world is become a shut book, which I do not wish to open for one word; and also on which soon the brass fastenings will be closed."

"With God looking on and pitying, and ——"

"Yes, now, for me, it is all being closed, ended. All life, to remember, feels nothing, and yet in passing it was such a struggle, such a succession of efforts, and sometimes such an intensity of thought. O the strictness of the habits with which I began my life in Manchester, and to which I made every thing bend, and by which I kept myself virtuous! O the disappointments I bore, the wrong I forgave! O the long, patient hours of study in an evening, year after year, by which I endeavored to compensate for the defectiveness of my education in a village school! O the triumphs I achieved against Toryism,— the way my name went about from mouth to mouth, and paper to paper, a watchword for the Liberals! O the multitudes who have listened to me breathless and convinced! In life, O the mountains I have crossed, the battles I have come through, the high places on which I have stood, with crowds thronging round me to applaud! But now that my path has turned from among men down into the valley of death, it feels to me as though, in all my life before, there had been no philanthropy, no integrity, no self-constraint, no public spirit, no success at all."

"Not, however," said the minister, "that there may not have been all these graces adorning our lives, as we walked along their course! And not that they do not exist still in reality! But at the end of life we are alone with God. And if we are right-minded, we cannot but feel that, with God watching us, our good actions are nothing to remember, and are even vanity. Can we, — would we wish to look at God, and be able to count up our own virtues while gazing at his holiness?"

"But are we not to believe that we are accepted for our righteous actions? And our past actions, are they not testimonies to us of what our life has been?"

"Myself," replied the minister, "myself, I hope for heaven, not for what virtue I can remember there having been in my actions, the best of them. But rather I hope for heaven because of that grace of God which teaches us that, denying worldly lusts, we should live soberly in this present world, looking for that blessed hope and the glorious appearing of the great God and our Saviour Jesus Christ."

"What, then, would you say moral actions are?"

"A way to the high hopes of religion; but not themselves hopeful merely out of their own nature."

"I am not sure that I understand you, sir."

"A right life," said the minister, "a right life I can only live with my face in the right direction. And at the end of this right life, it is not for me to be looking back for encouragement, but forward, up on high, to the Divine arms, which are reaching down toward me from heaven. And into our world, through the lips of Christ, O the blessed words God speaks! And if I have been walking right, my face must be in the right direction for catching them; and so I cannot fail of them, but hear them I must,— those words, blessed, blessed words,—'Come unto me, all ye that labor and are heavy-laden, and I will give you rest.'"

"Yes, I feel that, and I understand it," said Mr. Coke.

"You have a nephew, a student, I think, Mr. Coke."

"And you would wish me to send for him, now that I am ill. But I do not want to see him, even if I knew where he is, which I do not. I have known nothing of him for five years. And when I last saw him, he was every thing which

I am not, and which I hate and try to undo. He was a young Tory. Still I am obliged to you, Mr. Lingard, for your suggestion, because you meant it well. But just at present, with your permission, we will say no more about it."

## VIII.

The minister sat at his breakfast in his study. His cup of tea on the table was cold. On his knee there lay an open book; but he was not reading it. At last he rose from his chair, and said to himself, half aloud, "No, I cannot any way guess at it. Yet, quite certainly, on Mr. Coke's mind there is something which I ought to know of. There is some secret in him which he is the worse for keeping. What it is, how it is, I do not know. There is never a word of his I can fix on, which tells any thing. And yet sure I am, that on his mind there is something that overshadows it, blights it; for whenever he grows earnest, the voice of his soul sounds strange, and as though it were uttered from under something oppressive. A crime! One cannot suspect him of that; no, not for a moment. For he is the soul of honor incarnate. He might have sat with King Arthur among his knights at the Round Table. He is the only man of my knowledge whom Bayard would probably have liked, and whom Sidney might have called his friend. He is a noble figure and a noble mind. Along side of him, one's own soul erects itself, one's own heart beats firm and strong. I respect, — no, I do love him. Yes, I love him. For he has a large, tender heart in his breast, notwithstanding his austere expression and his authoritative way at times. A fine man, a true man, though proud! Pride, — ay, that is it! Whatever it is, that secret of his, — that miserable thing he keeps to himself, — it has something to do with his pride. It is his pride which has been the cause of it. But I must find it out. And yet I do not know how to get him to discover it. It would be ridiculous to think to extract a secret from a man like him. A frank, open question would be the proper and the likeliest way. But then his pride would be mortified at having let his secret trouble disclose itself. And then, if he did not answer my question, it would be worse with him, — his mental condition, — than it is now. What is that line on Chatterton? O, I remember, — 'The marvellous boy that perished in his pride.' Perish in his pride! That is what Mr. Coke might do.

He is a man to die of anguish with the serenest face. But what can it be, that should lie heavy on a mind like his? Strange! It is something his soul quails beneath, — a presence of terror about his mind. And they do not reach through it, as they ought, words of comfort or faith, nor even perhaps the gracious promises of the Gospel. What can it ever be? It has happened that a man has been haunted all his life by the face of a street beggar he had failed to relieve. But no; it cannot be any thing of that nature, — nothing merely fanciful. However, what it really is I shall learn soon, I trust. It is strange how we wrap ourselves about with folds of secrecy. And we are anxious to keep secret what is best in us, as much as what is worst. And we talk light things about the weather and outward life; and all the while in us our hearts are prompting earnest words. Life, — how often it is a monotony, a masquerade, with all the people in it dressed in drab, and dressed alike, and walking about and saying, 'How do you do? Very well, thank you.' A masquerade in dulness and drab, — this is what our social intercourse is often enough; instead of being a scene earnest with God's presence, and where angel thoughts pass from soul to soul. And myself, — how is it with me? It is just the same. And soon, my heart burning in me, and my lips quivering with emotion, I shall go down the street, and say to one and another, 'A fine day, sir. Good morning.'"

## IX.

In the early part of the evening Martin May called at the Parsonage. He had come up to it, past the cross, and through the town.

"Are the people," said he, "in this quiet place gone crazy? There are more vagabonds now in the square, than I thought there had been in all the country about."

"O, it is the wake," replied the minister.

"The wake, the wake! What is a wake?"

"In itself, it is what you saw, though in its history it is rather more respectable, perhaps. Though I suppose it has been a mere scene of debauchery for now more than three hundred years."

"Three hundred years! Is it so old, the folly?"

"The wake was once called a clerk-ale, or a church-ale, and was held on the festival day of the patron saint of the church, or perhaps on the eve of the feast. It was an entertainment given by the parish clerk, and was resorted to by all true lovers of the church, and perhaps of pastime. So that once this wake was a legal, an ecclesiastical institution,—or church-ale. As a reward for his services in the church, one day in the year the clerk was allowed to keep a tavern either in it or close by it. But now it is only an affair of the publicans, at their own houses, and for their own benefit. But still, in the celebration, it is the same thing now it used to be."

"And this is practised all over the country?"

"Yes, everywhere. And now you know what a wake is; and better than I do, perhaps: for I have avoided the sight for some years."

"At the Golden Lion, on long poles from the windows, there are hanging several hats, two gown-pieces, and a shawl. At the door there hangs a saddle and bridle and a profusion of ribbons. And on the top of the May-pole there is a hat."

"Those are the prizes for the winners at the games."

"And what are they?"

"Men in bags tied up at the chin, running races,—men blindfolded, running races with wheelbarrows,—donkey-races, at which the riders exchange animals amongst themselves, and the slowest wins, — women racing for gowns, — men grinning their ugliest through horse-collars, — boys eating hot hasty-pudding, with their hands tied behind them. And the hat on the top of the May-pole is the prize for climbing to it; the pole having been greased at the upper part. And by looking into the old authorities you will find that these are all ancient games, and no doubt once they were esteemed very humorous."

"But the drunkenness, the debauchery, that go with them!"

"The very thing your ancestor said, almost two hundred years ago."

"Did he? That is odd. But then, sir, how do you know he said so?"

"Because he was a Puritan. And to the Puritans these wakes were a great trouble and an utter abomination. Perhaps it was some pelting with stones at this very Thorpe wake, that determined your ancestor to emigrate. Even during the last century, at no time could a Presbyterian minister have walked through the square, on the day of the wake, without being assaulted with stones and worse missiles, as being a Nonconformist. Even I had to feel myself in some peril, once, close by the Cross, from people crazy for the day with drink and loyalty."

"Persecuted as a Puritan,—what would be the immediate causes that compelled my ancestor to follow the Pilgrims?"

"A heavy fine for every day's absence from St. John's Church,—and a very heavy fine, and perhaps imprisonment, for every time that he was caught praying along with a few of his neighbors, or listening to a Puritan clergyman. At Rivington there is a place where the Puritans of this neighborhood used often to meet in the night, or on a Sunday, for religious service."

"I must go to it."

"Almost it is an amphitheatre sunk in the top of a hill. And in it the congregation would meet and listen to some clergyman who was being persecuted from place to place. On all the ways leading to this spot there were stationed watchers against spies and the officers of the government. And perhaps some one of them would have a swift horse in his charge, for the clergyman to escape with. Because, if he were taken, he was severely punished, perhaps imprisoned for life."

"Well, I wonder they had not all gone out to the Colonies,—all the Puritans."

"And left England without the needful number of righteous men in it for its salvation!

For what would this town of Thorpe have been, if all the Puritans in it had gone out with your emigrating ancestor?"

"A spot of earth without any salt!"

"So it would have been, almost. And any time during the last century any body would have said so confidently."

"It is very interesting to me, sir, to see what the sources are in this Old England from which there have been derived to us in New England what is worthiest and most characteristic among us. And I find them chiefly among the Independents and the Presbyterians, as you call yourselves. In your graveyard, on an old tombstone, there is a name I have never seen nor heard anywhere else in England. But in Massachusetts it is a very common name. Were they to seek the source of their ancestral religion and character, the dwellers in three or four American towns, I fancy there would come thronging up to your church many thousands more than would get in."

"From a Presbyterian meeting-house, a few miles from this, half the congregation, with their minister, emigrated to America, at the latter end of the last century; being wearied out with persecution. I suppose a movement of that character was once common among the Puritans. And therefore, invisibly, but firmly, there are twined about our humble meeting-houses here roots that rise up in America, and meet together in the trunk of that tree of liberty, which now is grown so wide and high, as that all over the earth kings have sight of it, and beneath it, in its quiet shade, a great nation walks and works and rejoices. That is a metaphor, and would sound best in a speech. But also it is true; is not it? Well, have you discovered any other ancestor in your pious search of the register?"

"Yes, sir. I find that by an intermarriage there is some connection between me and one Sir Humphrey Coke. But who Sir Humphrey was I do not know. Do you think he was any ancestor of Mr. George Coke?"

"I cannot tell. Mr. Coke is a native of this neighborhood, but not, I think, of this place. But as for lineage, there is nobody knows what it may not prove for him, till he explores it. Only think that, five years ago, the descendant, the lineal representative, of the Nevilles, the great Earls of Warwick, the king-makers, was discovered by the lawyers sitting on a shoemaker's stall, at Northampton, all unconscious of his greatness."

## X.

The next morning after the preceding conversation, Martin May rode on the outside of the stage to Drayton, which is seven miles from Thorpe. He wanted to see the church there. "You will come upon it," said the coachman, "up that lane, just over the brow of the hill, and fifty yards beyond the stocks."

It was a long, low church, hidden in a dense mass of yew-trees. All round, the churchyard was thick set with yews, with only one narrow opening through them for a gate. For five hundred years and more must those trees have stood about the yard, thick, dark, and solemn. And inside them stood the church, mysterious, and looking as though there were lingering about it the shadows of centuries that were not yet quite over.

As it happened, the church was open. And

at the low door-way Martin May stooped and went in. In it every thing looked so ancient,— the benches for the poor,—the carved pews for the rich,—and the pulpit for the clergyman, with an inscription round it, in great gilt letters, denoting it to have been the gift of Dame Dorothy Scatcherd, more than two centuries ago. In the windows of stained glass were figures of the Apostles. But of all of them the heads had been broken out, and the holes been filled in with plain glass. On the opposite side of the chancel from the pulpit stood the font of stone, with a stone lid over it, suspended by a long rusty chain from the ceiling. Round the font, outside it, by some Catholic artist, were grotesque carvings of devils in trouble, from the holy water inside; one devil falling head over heels,—another grinning up at the spectator,—another catching at a child and missing it,—and another in his rage eating his own tail. In the chancel were numerous tablets to the Purefoys, a family which seemed to have been extinct for a century.

In one corner of the church, near the chancel, was a recumbent statue of Sir Humphrey Coke. By an inscription on the tomb, he was said to have been employed in many offices of trust, by Queen Elizabeth. And, beginning from the statue, there was a long range of tablets on the wall, ending with one, very simple and plain, to the memory of Mr. George Coke, farmer. "The history and decline of the Cokes," said Martin May, "it is all here, plainly enough. Why, the cost of that Sir Humphrey's marble statue would almost now be a fortune for one of his descendants; if, indeed, there are any of them living. And I wonder whether there are."

Just then came in the sexton. He was a man with a low forehead and a wide mouth; and he wore a brown smock-frock. Martin May said to him, "An ancient family, — these Purefoys! Is it in existence now?"

"I do not know where that is," answered the sexton. "If it were anywhere hereabouts, mayhap I could tell. Existence! Is it a borough, or a parish, or something of a hall? I have never heard tell of it."

"O, existence is a very wide, wide parish."

"Ah!" said the sexton, reflectingly. "How many funerals a week, now, may there be in it?"

"Innumerable."

"I never heard of that number before. Innumerable! Ah, we do not reckon that way in a little place like this. Do you know the sexton, sir, what his name is?"

"It is Time."

"And does he dig all the graves himself?"

"One by one, he himself buries every body."

"Well, now I get only a shilling for a grave. No more. And down by Thompson's tomb it is hard digging, very. But in those large parishes, especially in towns, there is better payment than there is in a little place like this. Now that Master Time, — what do you think he gets?"

"He gets it all his own way, all over the parish, with every body."

"Ah, does he? Then I will be bound that he is clerk as well as sexton."

"And so he is. And he says Amen at the end of every body."

"Ah," said the sexton, enviously, "when a man is clerk it goes well with him. He is not afraid, then, of the church-wardens. Not he! They cannot touch him any more than the parson. I should have been clerk myself; only they said I could not read. But Jim Stubbs, that is clerk, does not read much better than I can. And I could have got young Smithells to whisper me just as Stubbs does. And I am not hard of hearing, as he is."

"And so there are none of these Purefoys in Drayton now? And you have never known any thing of them?"

"No! They must have left the parish before my time. There has never one of them been a piece of work for me."

"Martin May looked up at one of the tablets in the chancel, and read aloud, — "Sir Percy Purefoy, — Hargham Hall."

"Hargham Hall," exclaimed the sexton, "that is close by. It is where the Purefights used to live a long while ago. When I was a boy, the old people used to talk about them. But nobody does now. Why they were called Purefights was because of that stone man in the corner. Not that one, but that other yonder! Seeing is knowing, they say. And you can see for yourself that he has his sword by his side, and his legs crossed, and his hands, as though he were praying. And that is the reason of the name. And all the family after him were called Purefights. So you see, sir, that any body who has ever lived in this parish I know about. But people in other parishes are no business of mine. Though sometimes there will come a funeral here out of some other parish. Because it is pleasant ground to lie in, — this of ours, — dry and wholesome. And that is what I ought to know, for I have dug down into it twelve feet deep. Twelve feet deep once, when it was snow-ing, I went down, and never took cold. And so I can say that it is a dry, comfortable spot for a body to lie in."

"Does the vicar live near?"

"Yes, sir; but he is not at home now. Nor is Jim Stubbs, that is the clerk. But if you want them, I will let them know. But a gentleman like you will not want to have the banns put up to be read. And if you have got the license, the curate at Harling will come over and marry you at any time."

"Not so fast, Mr. Sexton! I am not in need of your vicar's services at all. And if I were expecting so to be, I should rather they were going to be such services as you would yourself share in."

"That is very kind of you, sir," said the sexton, lifting his hand to the place where the rim of his round hat would have been, if he had had it on.

"But I belong as yet to the wide parish of Existence. And invisibly, yet I hope quite certainly, there are round about me the walls of the Church of Christ. And sometimes there are thundered at me sermons from on high, higher than this pulpit; and at other times there are such soft, sweet words for my hearing, that my soul in me melts at them. And these discourses I have to listen to for some time yet, I hope. And then at last that sexton Time will dig my place for me somewhere."

"Would not you like, sir, to come into the vestry?"

In the vestry, on a shelf, were a few books. And one of them was a volume of Fox's Book of Martyrs, with the chain yet hanging to it, by which it was once fastened in some public place for public reading, agreeably to an act of Parliament of the reign of Elizabeth.

While Martin May was looking at this old volume, a lady came in at the vestry-door. But on seeing a stranger there, she retired quickly. In the door-way she dropped her purse. Martin May picked it up, and half way down the aisle overtook the owner, and restored it to her, and said, "I shall be very sorry if I hinder your business here. I have none myself; and I am just now leaving. Will you excuse me? I should like to ask you one question, about these tablets; because it would be useless for me to inquire of the sexton. Are there any of this family of Coke surviving now?"

"Yes, one or two."

"And belonging to Manchester, either of them?"

"I think so — perhaps — yes. But I have been a stranger here for many years."

"Mr. George Coke, who has some connection with Thorpe, and who is very ill there just now; is he one?"

"I suppose so," said the lady, faintly, and sat down on one of the benches.

Martin May returned to the vestry for his hat. The lady was dressed in deep mourning. She was between thirty and forty years of age. Her voice was expressive of melancholy and great tenderness. While speaking, she had a very sweet smile. But it seemed as though commonly she might have that irresolute, absent look, which belongs to those persons who have long had their life of thought separated from their life of action.

The lady had dropped her veil before her face, while Martin May was in the vestry. He was returning down the aisle, and was bowing to the lady, as he passed, when she addressed him in a hesitating way, "You said, sir, that he — that the gentleman — that Mr. George was at Thorpe, ill."

"Yes, ma'am, very ill he has been. Though now he is getting better; and will recover, it is said."

"Thank you, sir. I am obliged to you for your politeness."

Martin May passed on, and went out of the church, unknowing of what he had done. When he emerged from the low portal into the sunshine, and stood among the graves that were fenced round by the ancient yew-trees so sombre and dense, he said to himself, "They rot here, one on the top of another, perhaps thirty generations of people, — men of yesterday, and also men of long ago, — valiant archers, to whom these yew-trees yielded bows for the fight and then shadows for their graves. And yet, with slight differences, it is the same thing over and over again, our human life."

He looked up at the dial over the church-door, and he saw by the index that it was exactly mid-day. And then he noticed that, sculptured in stone, outside of the dial, and coiled round it, there was drawn a serpent, the old symbol of eternity. And he said, "Yes, it is as Mr. Lingard says. Our lives are rounded by eternity, and to be perfected so. And shone upon by the Sun of Righteousness, always on the dial of life the index points to the hours, and also beyond them, and into infinity. Courage, my soul, courage!"

## XI.

At night Mr. Coke had a dream. He dreamed he was out of doors at midnight, sitting on a rock, and trying to pray, but unable to. Pray he could not; but could only think strange, wild thoughts of God. At last he stood up with tears on his face. And he cried in agony, "O God, I cannot pray. And if I bow down at the steps of thy throne, and lay hold of them, it is only to have my heart harden in me and blaspheme, in spite of my will. O, strike conviction into me, though it be ever so awfully, my God, my God!"

Then suddenly, from out of a fiery opening in the sky above him, there darted lightning. He raised his hand towards it, as though to accept God's answer to him, awful as it seemed. But in its swift descent the fiery shaft curled into a circle, and fell upon his head, and rested on it, like a crown of glory.

Then from underneath him the ground was lifted up. And all things round him were light; and things afar off were as plain to see as those close by him. And from his eminence he could see a long track: and it was that of his walk in life. And as he looked along it, there seemed to arise from along side of it things that were all formless, only that they could spread wings to hover on. And sometimes they seemed dark, and sometimes as white as light. But at last, altogether, they all appeared like forms of brightness. And then from one place and another they cried aloud, "We are the accidents you have undergone in life. We cursed you once, but now we bless." And then from all along the path, like one voice, they cried, "But now we bless."

And then the dreamer knelt and worshipped God. And his soul felt as though pervaded with infinite trust. And with his great joy he awoke. But even when he was awake, it felt to him as though his soul had been realizing other than human relationships. And there remained on his mind a feeling of wonder and solemn expectation.

## XII.

On the first day of September the minister sat with Mr. Coke.

" Thank you, Mr. Lingard. You are very kind. Will you ring the bell? Mrs. Gentle shall put the flowers into water."

" A curious inkstand, this!"

" I had it when a school-boy,—a gift from my father. And I believe once it was my grandfather's. You look surprised; and you wonder I have not a new inkstand every year,—a Reformer like me. But that quotation of yours yesterday, about understanding a character by some trifle,—it is not true. Our souls do not open like blossoms: and indeed they are not flowers at all. You are something of a botanist, and you can guess at a blossom from a single leaf. But you cannot divine a character from a word, one action, or a single trait."

"Why, no! For certainly I should have said this old inkstand was a testimony of your conservatism."

"And what does it mean, that for years that inkstand has stood on my dressing-table; and that now I have it in the parlor?"

"In sickness often I notice that thoughts of the past come thronging on a man, sweet and beautiful and welcome. And so I suppose it means ——"

"It is the only inkstand I have got. Because yesterday my other one was broken. Pardon my interrupting you. You had just said a true thing; and you were going on to something perhaps false."

"That new volume, — you have been reading it? What is it?"

"Nothing. I have just looked into it; and I see it is nothing. Of books of sentiment there are very few I can read now. Can you tell me why?"

"I suppose it is because now you are so earnest, and they are not."

"Shakspeare, — do you call him earnest? For even now I read him with as much satisfaction as almost any author. But while I say this, I am not unmindful of the Scriptures. For

I think the Bible is very properly not called a book, but the Bible, the book. The reasons for this you know better than I do. Myself, I can only say what I feel. And I say that the Old Testament transcends Shakspeare, more than the great dramatist does a mob of writers. And I believe I should feel this, and say it, even if I were a Hindoo, or a French infidel, the son of an infidel."

"I am glad to hear you say so," said the minister. "I mean that I am glad to have my judgment in one respect confirmed by the opinion of a man of your character, — a merchant and a politician, and not a theologian. It is held out to me by a hand from heaven, — the Bible. And so always there is on my soul a Divine awe, as I read it. But yet I think, did it lie on my table for me to peruse only like any other book, I should feel that it was so much superior to Plato or Shakspeare as to be still The Book. Because the various portions of it, even for mere style, are so good, so wonderfully good. Pen and ink now do not suffice for such a transcript of the soul. In reading Isaiah, I think sometimes I have his likeness, as though in a crystal well, which he was bending over with his prophet's eyes to search. And the Psalms, — they are living piety, and not merely the prayers and meditations of dead men. You can now even hear David's voice in them sobbing and mourning, and growing firm and clear, and at last joyous. O, it is very wonderful!"

"It is," said Mr. Coke, "and I have felt it so latterly more than ever in my life before. I think, sir, in sickness, one gets an ear, some inward ear opened. It would seem to be so with myself. And to this inward ear of mine many and many a popular book is dumb, speechless; and so is what I cannot read."

"A circumstance," said the minister, "a circumstance that is significant for the soul of the new world she is growing heir to. And it suggests, sir, does not it, that a man ought to set himself right with his fellow-creatures, and in all his earthly relations, when he knows by his feelings that he will soon cease to be of the earth."

"What do you mean; that I ought to make my will? I have done it. For I am not so foolish as to delay making my will till I should be likely to dictate it on the prompting of some nurse, or some whim, or some sick prejudice. I have made my will."

"And forgiven your enemies?"

"I have none that I know of, — not enemies.

For it is not me my opponents hate, but my politics, my work."

"I had fancied," said the minister, "you might have had much to forgive, very likely. Why I thought so I do not know. But I am glad I have been mistaken, — very glad."

"Well now, what else have you fancied in me, and then found you were mistaken in it? I should like to know, as a matter of curiosity."

"A self-accusing state of mind, betokened, I have thought, by a suppressed groan now and then, a look I could not account for, and now and then by some sentiment, which did not sound from you like the merely pious expression of humility it might have been in the mouth of some other person."

"Well, and on further knowledge of me ——"

"I seem to have been mistaken altogether, and never more thoroughly so in my life."

"Shall I trouble you to shut the door, Mr. Lingard? I am growing old in my legs, or else very young; for they do not carry me well now."

"You are always so cheerful with your illness."

"But really I feel impatience only too often. And do not you ever detect it?"

"Never, in word, or gesture, or tone. Never once have I heard you complain."

"Complain! No. And no merit in me, either. Me! It is not for me to complain of sickness, — this suffering. O God, not for me! Even the gentle relief there is in a sigh, is what I have no right to. Not I! Ah no! Complaint, — in me it would be a sin there is no word for; at least none that I know of. A sin there is no word for! And yet, Mr. Lingard, in me there is room for it."

"But not admission. That I am sure of. Though I will confess I do not understand you."

"And yet it would seem that once you thought you did. But for my part, I do not know myself. Circumstances, — some noticeable action, — a period of life, — a position, — will offer you the look of a man, just as a mirror will. But the man himself is invisible, aback of his actions and his looks. I look in the glass; and I see myself? O, no! I see a form once straight and strong, and a face rather long and sad; austere perhaps ——"

"And not unmajestic."

"And eyes dark and resolute —— "

"And earnest. And now and then there is an expression on your face, transient and strangely spiritual, and betokening that, while looking at your leger, your thoughts are not uniformly of merchandise."

"Ah! you would say it meant what?"

"That there is something earnest, some recollection or hope that passes through your mind often, but whether always without pain I do not know. Nay, it may be I ought to know. Pardon me: for I did not mean to distress you. And I am sure I must have said something wrong."

This the minister said by way of letting the sick man recover from his emotion. And for the same reason he continued thus: "But, indeed, with much reading I have forgotten well how to talk. And perhaps I have lost something of discernment and discretion that might have been serviceable among my friends, because, as Roger Ascham said of himself, I have been a looker-on in the cockpit of learning these many years. But I hope you will pardon me, Mr. Coke, if I have said any thing to pain you; for it has not been intentionally."

"There is a subject, Mr. Lingard, on which I wish to speak to you: and I will do so just now. You have my confidence. And my heart has wanted to speak to you when you have uncovered it, as more than once you have, in talking with me. Ah, no, Mr. Lingard, we do not know one another, even when we think we do, most intimately. You know this wasted frame of mine, and my voice, and what is occasionally my abrupt manner. But you do not know what fountains of feeling, once copious, are now sealed in me. To the outward world I am resolute, decisive: but in the inner world I am surrounded with terrors, and awful recollections, and memories that are like the ghosts of dead hopes, and words that sound unendurably. And sometimes among these I am not what I am on the exchange or the platform, but a poor creature,—a creature of misgivings and fears and griefs."

"Often," said the minister, "it would be better for every man, were the inmost chamber of his thoughts thrown open to some friend. For sometimes it happens, that in our minds there will harbor unreasonable fancies, terrific notions, of which a friend would free us with a word, though ourselves we may be quite impotent against them."

"So I think."

"As Pythagoras said, eat not thy heart. It is ill food, and suicidal. You stare; but indeed it is suicidal, as I could show you by many examples, and from the nature of the soul as social. I remember something of Bacon's. It is to this effect:—You may take sarza to open the liver, and prepared steel to open the lungs, and castor for the brain; but for opening the obstructions of the heart, there is no medicine found besides a faithful friend, to whom you may impart griefs, joys, fears, hopes, suspicions, and cares, under the secrecy, as it were, of a confession."

"Your reading has been to good purpose, Mr. Lingard. It serves you well. I was thinking so, yesterday. It seems as though always there were a ghostly library about you, from the invisible shelves of which memory reaches you any book you want, open at the right place for quoting."

"O, do you think so?"

"You have lived very much alone, yet you know men well. And this town is but a quiet place; and you seldom go out of it."

"But I have my own heart to talk with. And one time, the flesh prompts me; and another time, the Holy Spirit enlightens me. And always within sight there are men and women and children for me to watch. Yet it is a quiet town, this. Though it might be much smaller than it is, and yet yield more wisdom than the city, with its vastness and excitement and fresh news every day. Said Sir Thomas Palmer, when he was brought out on to the scaffold, 'I have learned more in a dark corner of the Tower, than in travelling round Europe.'"

"Well said!"

"It is true not only of books, but also of the ways of the city, those of business and manners, as Selden said, that no man is the wiser for learning."

"Good!"

"It is a small place, — this town. But I can say that, like Fletcher of Madeley, I have an advantage here, which I could not have to a similar degree in a larger place. For as he said of himself to a friend, so I say to you, that my little field of action is just at my door; so that, if I happen to overdo myself, I have but a step from my pulpit to my bed, and from my bed to my grave."

"That is pleasantly, sweetly said."

"Here, in this town, we live along side of our graves. But in the city it is otherwise. Indeed, I know some towns a man might live in and never see a grave. But in this little town, here are two graveyards, — spots of awful silence among us, — solemn, thoughtful places to walk in. As you know, I myself live along side the graveyard. But, as I was going to say, I think it is a virtuous help to have it made visible how close against the grave is every man's walk in life."

"Mr. Lingard," said Mr. Coke, in a trembling voice, "I am dying by a death that is not quite free from the guilt of suicide."

"Suicide! Not that! You cannot mean that. My dear sir, you are dying of consumption; as I have long supposed you would. But you are very feverish; are not you, very?"

"No, I am not; not at all. O merciful God, be merciful to me."

"That you said just now, you were dying of ——"

"Was — was suicide. There! I have said it once more. Lord, have mercy on me!"

"Mr. Coke, tell me what you mean," said the minister in a soothing tone.

"Ten years ago I was engaged to a lady to be married."

"And the lady died?"

"No, she is living now. I was in business in Manchester, not as a partner with others, but altogether on my own account. Through years of adversity, at last I had risen into a prosperous position. One morning, — it was a Saturday, — a dull, foggy day in February, — I remember it all so well, — how it was the middle of the day, and the gas was lit, — how my desk stood, — and how there lay on it a book, and four or five letters, and a sample of cotton,—and how there came to me a merchant. He gave me his name. I remembered to have heard it before. For testimony as to his trustworthiness, he referred me to a mercantile company of some eminence, and till then of high character. By them I was induced to execute for the man a large order for goods. It was a swindling transaction. And in two days I knew that I was a ruined man."

"A ruined merchant, Mr. Coke, but not a ruined man; that you never could have been."

"Ah, the old mistake again! But I made it in a worse way before. I felt myself a ruined man, or my pride did. And so—and so —— On Thursday I met the father of my betrothed. There was conversation between us. How it reached the conclusion I do not know. But it was this,—that I was too poor for his daughter. About ten days afterwards I received a letter from him, in which he complimented me on my honorable conduct, and said he supposed I should be glad to learn that his daughter had quite recovered her cheerfulness, although for two or three days she had been distressed at the position in which she had been placed by my misfortune. With that letter I became desperate. There was not a human being I cared for. Such a silent scorn as I had even for the kind words of my friends! Though, indeed, they were not many. I became impatient of life. I was travelling, and I got wet through. At night I laid my clothes beside my bed, and in the morning I put them on, wet as they were. That morning I said no prayer. A godless, reckless day it was! I knew what I was doing; for I believed that I might perhaps be bringing on my death. And from that time to this I have been in a consumption. All these years!"

"Years of repentance, I know they have been, — must have been, — a repentance that has been acceptance with God, I am sure."

"Not a morning or evening ever since, but I have prayed to be forgiven. And I trust I am forgiven. Through Christ I must hope so, must believe so, and am bound to think so. But oh! it clings to me, — the awful recollection. And it disgusts me with myself. That crime, — I cannot undo it, I cannot wipe it from my history. And it is on me and with me for ever."

Here the minister rose and walked across the room two or three times.

"I see," said the sick man, "I see I have surprised you with my confession, and perhaps revolted you. But what I have said I wanted to speak to you, for I have never uttered it yet any way but in prayer. But you are surprised —— "

"Well, I am so; but even more at your tears than your words. For I was not sure you could weep."

"In all my life, this sin was the first thing I ever wept for. No disappointment, nor loss, nor bereavement, nor unfaithful friend, but only this sin first drew tears from me."

"And so drew you to be human. And was it not so, that with those first tears you felt yourself another creature? Easily I can tell what you were once. Innocent and proud of your innocence, — erect both in body and mind, and haughty, — free from every weakness yourself, and impatient of it in others, — so correct that you had no consciousness of sin, — and — shall I say it? — so self-righteous, you felt no abasement before God's holy eye, and little need of Jesus as a Mediator! Strong, and resolute, and moral, and self-confident, you walked the world, listening to the echoes of your own footsteps, — without sin almost, and almost without God in the world. I say it was so; was it not?"

"I am afraid it was. And indeed you have been correctly informed."

"Informed! Not I! But of myself I can well suppose what you must have been once,—before that voice of yours had ever trembled with misery or prayer."

"God pardon me! I trust he will. Because, for years and years, it has been my prayer every day, and at some seasons every hour of the day, almost. And sometimes I have thought it was forgiven me,—this sin. But then, again, at other times it would seem so hateful, horrid,—this recollection of sin clinging to me."

"Pride, pride! Mr. Coke, in your state of feeling on this matter, there is not a little pride. Fain would man be self-righteous, unknowing of this,—that there is a higher virtue than can altogether begin and be sustained from within his own heart,—the holiness of a soul that has gone through sin into the sense of infinite need, and so forward to Christ and salvation by grace."

"There seems a black cloud moving off my soul. And this instant I am happier than I have been for ten years. But O, sir, that day, that reckless, wicked day! I must not wish it blotted out of my life, I suppose. But O my misery at that time! Out in the street, it was as though every body were looking at me as a ruined man. And by the fireside, all the sweet thoughts I had had for months seemed to mock me, every one of them. From behind, the past pressed against me, like a weight of misery; and before me, the future was darkness there seemed no way to walk in. And so that action, — that wickedness that was not without a thought of self-murder ——"

"Nay, nay," said the minister, "do not call it so, Mr. Coke, I will not have you call it so. Though I would not have you extenuate the guilt of it. Yet I suppose it would not have happened had she been true to you, — your — I mean your betrothed."

"She was not otherwise than true. O, do not blame her. I never have for a moment, or in one thought. Whatever was blamable, if any thing were, was between me and her father; and perhaps it was more with me than him, or even altogether with me. My pride, — I do not know how it spoke, nor what it said. All I remember is the spot I stood on, and the weight of woe that fell upon me, as he, her father, turned and left me. It was woe on woe upon me, and intolerable I thought. Yet what was it? It was nothing, almost nothing as a weight to what has borne upon me since, walking or sitting, — this — this remembrance of what I have told you. There is seldom a morning, on my waking, but this comes to me horrid and fresh, as though it were yesterday's wickedness."

"Will you have a little water, Mr. Coke? You remember what I said about your being led to Christ and holiness, through first being convinced of sin. I would ask you to think of it, — and also I could wish you to read one or two pages of St. Augustine. In some features of character I think you may resemble him. A Manichean once, and a wanderer in sin and sophistry for fifteen years, he became at last a Christian and a bishop. By the Catholic Church he has been canonized as a saint, and been reckoned one of the four great doctors. And by painters he has had given him for his symbol a flaming heart."

"Patience with our sins, — I have heard of that phrase. And I think I begin to discern some meaning in it."

The minister continued, "Temptation, sin, remorse, an agony of helplessness, then Christ as a resource, repentance, and reconciliation to God, — that is the process which many a soul goes through, and by which often it proves that the

Christian Stoic becomes Christian truly, and has his soul grow in grace, and open freshly and largely into the feelings of revĕrence, awe, and mystery, trust and love, patience, resignation and hope. There is a sense in which it may be said that Christianity begins from the consciousness of sin. And that feeling most commonly begins from some particular act; though it may, and with some persons it does, rise in the heart of itself, — as though from a man's hating himself for what he must look in the eye of God. The consciousness of sin, — a dark and awful passage, — not without lightnings that flash in it, and terrible voices that whisper and roar along it, and dishearten and distract and appall! But it emerges in a serene region of lowliest worship and loftiest virtue."

## XIII.

Sarah Burtenshaw had arrived in London and been domesticated there a little while, when there arrived the following letter, addressed to Mrs. Satterthwaite at the Parsonage: —

"I write to you, with my best respects. I got to London quite safely. O, what a large place it is! And there is such a noise! And there are carts and coaches and omnibuses, more than I should have thought there had been in all the world. But the most wonderful thing of all is, that you put your ashes and sweepings out at the door, and there comes a dustman and takes them away in his cart. And no trouble to you at all! In our house there is a lodger. And he is so like Mr. Coke, only smaller, that I think he must be his brother. But it seems astonishing, all this way off, to meet with any body one had ever known before. Not that I had ever known Mr.

Coke before; for I had not. O, I forgot to say, his name is Coke. Such a sweet, good gentleman! And he does nothing at all but read. And such a quantity of books he has! Almost as many as the minister! From what I heard my master telling some one at dinner once, I suppose he was to have been a clergyman. But he would not take orders. But I should not have thought he would have minded doing that, as he is a very quiet gentleman. But nobody likes being ordered about, at first, I suppose; though afterwards it comes easier. Some time when I have got to know him better, I shall ask him whether he knows any body at Thorpe. But at present I am afraid to. I often think of what you told me. And I remember the minister every time I see the workbox. And often I pray for him, at night, as I ought to. I try not to think about it, else often I should cry, because I cannot be at Thorpe. London is a very grand place, but home is home, though it be ever so homely. I should often wish I could come and see you, in an evening; but, as father often said, wishes never can fill a sack. Though I hope it is all for my good."

This letter Mrs. Satterthwaite took up stairs to the minister in his study. She saw that he had a pen in his hand, and was occupied with thought, so she laid the letter on the table beside his desk, and retired without speaking.

## XIV.

Again the minister sat at his breakfast-table: and again his cup of tea was cold. Again he had lying upon his knee some book, which he was not reading. And again he rose from his chair, and talked with himself, half aloud. "It haunts me, — does this confession of Mr. Coke's. All day yesterday it was with me. I was thinking of it last night, when I went to sleep; and on my waking, this morning, it was the first thing which came into my mind. Those woful tones, how they linger in my ears! And what a sight it was, — a man weeping, — a proud man, and a proud-looking man! That wrong action which he confessed, I suppose, might almost be called his one sin; only that our human nature is so permeated with sin, often latent perhaps, but with every body, one way or another, so certain to break out into action.

But now as to Mr. Coke. He does not think about this sin rightly, though with the bitterest repentance. From his character and his manner of thinking, it is very certain that he supposes his sin to be something which he has drawn down upon his head, and not what it really is, — a something which has been developed out of his own heart, essence of his essence, and nature of his nature. A nature all miserable but for the Saviour, by whom we have redemption! As to the sincerity of his repentance, there can be no doubt. And O what he must have passed through, in the seasons of this long illness, and the lonely hours he has had! I pity him. And yet no; it is scarcely pity that I feel. But I love him truly, and all the more, the more I know of him. And he, — strange, rare exception to sinners, — almost he needs to learn to compassionate himself. A blighted life! Who would have thought that of him, who had seen him five years ago, courageous, calm, and dignified? With men in awe of him, — subduing a mob by the tones of his voice, — and frightening corrupt men with his glance; who would have thought that himself he was trembling with a recollection, and quailing at a thought? A noble man, and all the dearer to my regards, if not for that one error of his, yet certainly for what has followed on it, — his agony of remorse, — his broken pride, — and his eye for the spiritual growing more and more clear, and yet more and more abashed and awe-struck. O, if only we knew one another better! Would it be to love one another less? I think not, but rather more tenderly. But would it be possible for us to understand one another? Could a peasant understand a poet, his fears and hopes, his raptures and dislikes? No, he could not. And how would it be, at times were we accompanied by forms emblematic of the chief virtues and vices of our lives? Myself how should I appear? To my people, how should I look preaching from among an airy cloud of faithful emblems? O, for that I should need a congregation of other hearers than men, — not Walter Floresman with his quick sense of inconsistencies, nor John Lake with his impatience of improprieties, nor any little child in its innocence and its healthy horror of sin. For the sake of my people, O that I might sanctify myself, as well as inform myself. These books about me, all these books have I provided, that by them I may get knowledge. But for holiness how am I striving? And, indeed, without holiness there is no knowledge, no real knowledge of the human heart. And without it how shall I speak to men's souls? For though without holiness I can delight men, and give them information, and be eloquent in their ears; yet unless myself I am holy, I cannot save them, cannot help them much towards salvation."

## XV.

One evening Martin May sat on a stile, under an oak-tree, by the side of the highway. And along the road came Justice Burleigh in a gig, with his coachman driving him.

The gig stopped opposite the stile. And the Justice called out, in a fierce tone, "Are you the Yankee that is staying about here?"

"Yes, I am," answered Martin May, very gently.

"Then what do you mean by telling people that every body can go a poaching over in that country of yours, wherever it is?"

"I never said so."

"O, you did not? What did you say, then?"

"Well, I was talking with some farmers, one evening, and I said that in America there was no such thing as poaching. And I believe I may have said, that it would be a shame if there were."

"Eh, what! No poaching in America!" exclaimed the Justice, quite mollified in his tone. "What lies people tell! Good country magistrates, eh? Active, eh? Good, strict laws against the possession of fire-arms, eh? But no poaching, — no poaching at all?"

"None whatever. For a farmer, on his own ground, it is all fair, open shooting, because there is no game-law against it. On his own land, at proper times, without leave or license from any quarter, a man can kill his own woodcocks and eat them, his own partridges, his own quails ——"

Here the Justice went crimson in the face, and half rose in the gig, and cried, "His own, — your own, — his own! Who told you they were his own? Sir, who are you to find fault with this country? What have we to do with your outlandish notions? A vagrant, for all your looks! Ay, my fine gentleman, you may laugh, but I have committed better looking men than you before now. Let me catch you trespassing or shooting, and then you shall see, or my name is not Burleigh. A pest of a fellow! You to be pretending flaws ——"

Here the Justice choked with rage. And here Martin May rose from his seat, and advanced a step, and said, in a quiet tone, "Flaw! There is something of a flaw in your title to Haslingden. And I can make it good with a name I have discovered. I tell you, because you are a kinsman of mine; though not very near, I am glad to say."

Here the Justice drove off without a word. However, in a few days he sent one of his gamekeepers to the Dell, with a present of a brace of pheasants and another of partridges.

## XVI.

One afternoon the minister sat with Mr. Coke, and after some conversation with him on sin and its pardon through Christ, he said, "A man grown humble with his sin, and a man sinfully proud of his innocence, — they are both sinners before God. But perhaps the one will be saved through Christ, and possibly the other may never even learn that he needs saving."

"But," said Mr. Coke with a groan, "that wilful act of mine, — it feels so unlike any other sin! It is not that I do not believe in the grace of God! Not that I have not faith in the Lamb of God as taking away the sins of the world! But somehow I feel as though this sin of mine were something by itself. I suppose my feeling about it is something morbid, from my having kept it to myself so long. It is as though it were a sin unlike and beyond other sins; and as though by it there had been a line drawn about me, between me and the common world. A sin of blood or temper or pressing circumstance,—but then it was not of that nature."

The minister did not know well how to answer. For he did not think it right ever to attempt to diminish in any one the sense of sin. And yet he felt that properly something ought to be said of a soothing nature,—some explanation, or sentiment, or some quieting text from Scripture. He leaned back in his chair a few moments, in silence; and then he began to speak in a manner like soliloquy. "When reason fails a man in despair, it is very dreadful; but I do not know that really it should be sadder than when reason fails an angry man in his passion; and very certainly it is not so sad as when reason fails a covetous man, and lets him live a mere money-getter; and it may be much less sad than when reason fails a man in his love of pleasure, and lets him grow to be an old sensualist."

Here the sick man wiped from his eyes some tears which had started to them. The minister continued, "There are some of the very happiest persons, who cannot stand on a rock, nor look down from a church-steeple, without wishing to throw themselves headlong. And there are some high contemplations, on ascending into which, some purest souls could wish themselves perished, annihilated. This is strange: but so also is our whole nature, as soon as it is seriously thought of. Perhaps it is no very great wonder, that now and then reason should fail one of us utterly. For it is an event which has been left possible, in God's making of the world and us. Indeed, it is for the trial of our minds that very largely the world is what it is."

The minister ceased for a moment, and then continued, in a manner from which almost it might have seemed that he had been unconscious of there being any one present with him, "Fearful and wonderful is this nature of ours, — flesh and spirit both, — body dwelt in by soul! A person is master of other men, and of circumstances, and almost of the elements, sometimes through being nervously excited a little; but let that little excitement with him be only a little more, and then he is not master even of his own faculties. A man is himself one moment, and the next moment he is not himself; and perhaps this difference is from a grain of sand, or from one drop of blood, pressing against a nerve, itself too small even to be seen. At one time, thought flashes in the mind, like lightning out of heaven;

and at another time it is all darkness in the mind, and merely from the brain being a little torpid. A man will be troubled, day by day, and one year after another, and be cheerful the whole while, as long as he is healthy. But let him be ill, and then he will be crushed by perhaps the lightest of his former afflictions. A sudden noise, a moth in the dark, some old word heard anew, a curious coincidence of trifles, — even these little things will startle us. So that it is not astonishing that sometimes self-possession should quite fail one of us. Because itself the world is more awful than any one of us has ever felt it. There are shadows from infinity fallen upon it; although commonly they are walked in without being recognized; so that, when there is sudden notice of them, it may well be awful."

"Yes," exclaimed Mr. Coke, "what a world it is that we live in! And what frail creatures we are that live in it!"

"Here and there," said the minister, "are such happy circumstances, as that a person born in them grows up almost as though in the garden of Eden, and knows the sorrows of life only like shadows passing over sunshiny meadows. And then it happens for the man, that with his first real sorrow he feels for the first time the sorrowfulness of the world itself as a dwelling-place. And so, perhaps without any great change of circumstances, the happy creature of one month is the next month a fellow-sufferer with the bereaved, and the oppressed, and the starving, and the sick, everywhere. And so for him all at once, instead of walks in the garden of Eden, the paths of the world feel as though leading only to sick-beds, and prisons, and graveyards. Simply by seeing one another, and talking with one another, we do not know one another. And often in our souls there are deeps up out of which no voice comes for others to hear, and down into which seldom do we look ourselves. And yet, after a long time, there may rise up thence involuntary thoughts, which we do not know how to reason with, from our having always been silent on the sources of their origin. And so I never see a good youth, who is sensitive as well as intellectual, but I could pray to God for him, against the secret perils of spiritual growth. For sometimes in such a person ways of feeling grow secretly, which are felt for the first time, and suddenly, only when they have become very strong."

"What comfort," said the sick man, "there is merely in the sound of another's sympathetic voice! And how wrong we often are, — we men,—in not availing ourselves of it! We are afraid of its being a weakness."

"Whereas it is nature and an ordinance of God. I doubt whether any man can comfort himself effectually. And even in their reasonable convictions, they are very few who can be alone and strong."

"That is true! Often and often I have had to notice it, especially in regard to persons living in small communities."

"If I would convince myself," said the minister, "would I convince myself, I must first persuade another man, and then have my own reasons speak to me from out of his mind. With persuading another, I get more thoroughly convinced myself. Mere speaking aloud does not suffice. A man may talk and talk, till he has talked away all his faith, if he talks merely from vanity or restlessness. On spiritual subjects a man must not speak into the air, but to the soul of another, or it will be the worse for him. Nor does the philosopher need a philosopher to sympathize with him. Quite otherwise. For he may grow clear in mind, and strengthen in faith, and grow joyful in his belief, with only talking to an unlettered man or a simple serving-woman, who knows no more than that she is very ignorant."

"Yes, Mr. Lingard, you are quite right. Though it is what we men, in our pride, do not often think."

"And so I do not know but that sometimes others may benefit by the thoughts of an author more than he does himself, — be better strengthened and more effectually consoled for the dark, rough path of life, with the grave across it."

"And that, too, is one of the hard things the world abounds in! A man waters with his blood the tree of the knowledge of good and evil; and then upon it the most beautiful blossoms and the choicest fruit are not for himself, but for others, — persons of no self-sacrifice and not much thought."

"And," said the minister, "often all that is left him is to lie down beneath the wonderful tree and die, — and, dying so, to make others be more and more convinced of life immortal. On the moors I have noticed there are spots on which the snow will not lie, however deep it may be everywhere else about. And in this world there are some graves, standing on which we cannot grow cold with unbelief, as long only as we believe that God is just. They are the graves of the good and great, who have suffered, — who have hungered, and have not perhaps had even simple food yielded them, — who have yearned for higher love than met them in the world,—who have talked in a strain too nearly that of angels for many men to join them in it,—and who have been God's agents in the world for good,—immortal good,—they in their few years and many troubles. All this,—how forcibly one would feel it by the grave of Sir Thomas More or Andrew Marvel."

"Or at Lutterworth, where I once stood in Wicliff's church ——"

"But the troubles of the purest of us men,—what are they to the sufferings of Jesus Christ? They,—they are of high, infinite, eternal meaning. God letting his Son die for me; O his pity for me! God helping me through the death of his own Holy One,—searching after me through his Son as a spectacle on the cross,—and striving to soften me with his Son's agony;—O the way I ought to feel, so tender towards him, so patient with his dealings! God the unseen, trying to make his character visible by his Son dying, and in his Son's death;—O, shall I not understand him and believe? God calling me to look up at heaven, past and beyond the cross his Son hangs on;—shall I not feel it, and rejoice in it solemnly,—the hint, the intimation, the doctrine, I feel, that the way of the cross is that of glory?"

## XVII.

It was Saturday evening and towards sunset. Martin May sat on the bridge, close by the house at the Dell. There were many signs of the week nearing its end. The stage-coach went past; and then several market-carts. And some of the horses of the farm were taken over the bridge, on their way to the pasture for their Sunday's rest. And then there came along a wagon loaded with wheat. It was the last of the harvest; and so it was followed by several laborers in a kind of rural triumph. And among them was one who strode along in a white smock-frock, playing on a violin. Such a still, quiet evening it was! And already on his soul Martin May felt the calm of the coming Sunday. Close by him, flying about from one spot to another, a robin redbreast was singing that song of his, which sounds so cheerful in the winter and so pensive in the autumn. Martin May was listening to it, when he was startled by a man who approached him from behind, and said, " Sir, my name is Sharples, — Humphrey Sharples. And I have a letter for you. It is from our secretary; and he wants an answer. I have told him about you; and he knows you are a friend of liberty; and so he is willing to have you address our Association of the United Chartists and Friends of Humanity. And perhaps you would like to have me come and talk over the matter with you, to-morrow."

"No; not to-morrow, because it will be Sunday."

"O, I do not mind that. I have read too much for that, as well as you."

"O Mr. Sharples, but myself I have not read as much as that yet."

"But you will help us, sir, all the same?"

"Your secretary shall have my answer by the post," said Martin May, putting the letter in his pocket. "And you yourself I will help in any way that is in my power."

"Ay, I knew you would," said Mr. Sharples. "For I heard of how you answered Justice Burleigh, that evening. A man that was behind the hedge the while told me. He is one of the greatest tyrants, that man, sir. He belongs to the aristocracy. And so does almost every body about here. Only there is nobody quite as bad as he is, without it may be Sir Wilmot Wilmot, as they call him, or Parson Scoresby, or Squire Pickford, or Squire Horrocks, or Farmer Whigham, or Farmer Crankshaw, or Gornall, or Lawyer Steele, or Doctor Blinkhorn, or ——"

"Then Justice Burleigh is not the worst, by many."

"Any way," said Mr. Sharples, flushing in the face, and stretching out his right hand, "any way, he is an oppressor, and worse than Brutus."

"I do not remember to have heard of him before, in such connection. Brutus! Was he a cousin of Lord Castlereagh's?"

"Likely enough. Though as to his connections, I do not know any thing about them, and I do not care either. But no doubt he was some lord. I am not like some of the people about here. There is John Illingworth. He knows every thing about these Wilmots for hundreds of years, — what families they married into, — what battles they were in, — what offices they held, — and how some of them were beheaded in London. And that last is the best thing he has to say about them. So I tell him. And then he gets into a rage."

"But how comes he to know so much about them?"

"O, all the best of his life he was a servant of theirs; and so was his father, and his grandfather. And so is his son now. I tell him it is time there was a change,—time for him to have his turn at the castle. And that angers him terribly. And why it should I cannot think. But it shows how unreasonable a man becomes by living with the aristocracy. That is what I say, and do not you think so, sir?"

"Unreasonable! That depends on what you call reason. And so what is reason?"

"Reason is right,—having one's rights."

"Whose rights?"

"My own. For what have I to do with any body else's?"

"And Mr. Sharples, your rights are ——"

"Universal suffrage. And you know what that is; for you have it in America."

"Not universal. For a minor has not the suffrage."

"Well, a man is not obliged to be that, I suppose, and work in a pit. But for all other classes it is universal, is not it?"

"No. For women have no votes."

"Women! And why should they have? Besides I am not a woman. And if I were in America I should have my share in the government. And that is what we want you to show next Friday."

"And to show that in America the people are all educated?"

"Well; that is because of their having the suffrage."

"Yes; but also they acquired the suffrage through their having first been an educated people."

"O, I do not know about that."

"And no fault of yours either, Mr. Sharples. But as I was born among them, I do happen to know. Mr. Sharples, your conversation interests me very much. You have read ——"

"As much as any man I know about liberty, Cobbett and ——"

"You have learned to read and write? Then I want you to make me a list of such books or tracts as you think are good reading on the subject of English society."

"I will tell you them now."

"But I wish you to write them down for me, if you will. And I will pay you for your trouble."

"I cannot write; for I have never learned to. And that is the doing of the aristocracy."

"Never learned! But writing is taught in the free schools here."

"But it was not when I went to school. It was not at St. John's, which was the school I belonged to."

"But at the other school, — at that by the Presbyterian Chapel, — there was writing taught, twenty years ago, was there not?"

"Well, I believe there may have been. But I did not belong there. For at that time I used to go to church, along with my father. And he would have thought it a shame to go into a chapel, or to let me go to the Presbyterian school. But I have heard that once the Presbyterians were more zealous for liberty than almost any other people. But when the Charter was brought forward, the minister proved to be an aristocrat. And I was the man to detect him."

"Do you mean Mr. Lingard?"

"Yes, I do. The petition for the Charter, — I took it to him to sign. And he would not. And because he would not, others would not. And so there has never been a Chartist near his chapel since. Though to be sure there never were any Chartists used to attend there regularly. Myself I used to go there sometimes. But now I do not. For I take a book and go into the fields, and lie on the grass. And a very good way it is; for the country was made before the church."

"And Mr. Lingard was made before you. And so it might be well for you to go to him sometimes; might it not?"

"Sir," said Mr. Sharples, "I have no patience with any body that will not let me have my rights. It is all very well, — fine talk. But what right has Squire Burleigh to that great hall, and two or three carriages, and wine every day, while I have got nothing? What more right has he to these things than I have? That is what I asked Parson Lingard. It was a harder question than he had ever had put to him before, I know. It went deep down to the bottom of the matter: and he could not meet it. Sir, he could not answer it."

"I wish you would ask me," said Martin May, "and I will answer it."

"Well, I do ask you," said Mr. Sharples, in a tone half confident, half surly.

"Considered as pigs then, you and Justice Burleigh, he would have no better right to the hall than you. It is the end and fulfilment of a pig's nature to lie still and grow fat; and so it would be just as much the right of pig Sharples to grow fat in Haslingden Hall, as it would be of pig Burleigh. But, Mr. Sharples, you are not a pig, but a man, and a man of some fine qualities. And so the end of your life is not fat, but character, honesty. And now you can understand why you have no right to Haslingden Hall. If you were a pig, you might have some right to it, as a sty. But as a man, you have no right to the place; and as an honest man, you will feel you have none."

"Pooh! Is that all?"

"Cannot I make you understand? You do understand, Mr. Sharples. I am sure you do. There is no law for the pig against covetousness. But there is for man. Grovelling and walking on all fours, — head down, — the pig is following his whole true nature in following his mouth. But man is erect, — his head high up in the world. And from the soul in him, man is high enough to hear things of the spirit, — laws of a higher world than this of dust. It is man's distinction, sad and mournful sometimes, but always solemn and glorious, that he can hear what the brutes cannot, — what is Divine, and a commandment, — 'Thou shalt not covet.'"

It was growing dusk. Mr. Sharples was silent. And it seemed as though he might have been convinced. But he got down from the parapet of the bridge, on which he had been sitting, and replied, in a tone of bitterness and triumph, "That may be very well in America, where people have enough to eat. But do you think it sounds much to me, or ought it to? For I have had nothing to eat to-day."

"You!" exclaimed Martin May, quite horrified. "Nothing to eat! Had nothing to eat!"

"No," said Mr. Sharples, in a fierce, triumphant tone, "I have had nothing inside my lips all this blessed day. And now, sir, where are you? and where is your argument? I have done half a day's work; and I have walked fourteen miles; and I have not had a morsel to eat to-day. And now what have you to say about Justice Burleigh?"

"Nothing. I have nothing to answer you now. But come with me, and have something to eat."

"Not I!" said the other. "Not I! I am no beggar."

"No; but a poor, patient man. Come, come!" and Martin May drew him by the arm towards the house.

"I will not. I am no beggar. Not I!"

"Nor I a thief! I have had all this time of yours. And now I must pay you for it. Indeed I must, and I will."

"Hands off, sir! Let me go," said the Chartist, in a relenting tone.

"No, Mr. Sharples, no! You have got the better of the argument, you think. But you cannot throw me in a wrestle. So come along, and share my supper; or else I will call help to carry you. There! Come along."

In the house the table was set for supper. It was covered with bread, cheese, butter, bacon, beef, and pigeon-pie. Mr. Sharples was just going to begin his supper; and all his hungry body was in a tremor of expectation and delight. But there was set down, near his left hand, a silver tankard of ale. At the sight of this aristocratic object, his Chartism was aroused; and with the near neighborhood of it, he felt as though his principles were being compromised. He dropped his knife, pushed back his chair, and stood up and cried, "No, no! I have not tasted yet. I will have none of it. This is no place for me, — no place for me." And, bewildered and faint, he looked about him wildly. But the tall, round farmer rose beside him, and laid his great hands on his shoulders, and cried, "Down, fool, and eat a supper when you can get it! I say, Numps, be a man for once. Ho, ho, ho! Numpy, Numpy! Thou wert always for talk, talk, talk, instead of filling thy belly."

The farmer sat down again in his great arm-chair, and laid hold of the handle of the silver tankard, and looked round the table, and said, "Is every body served? Ay, Numpy, we will fill thee, for once, to-night. And we would have thee half drunk too, only that it is Sunday to-morrow. The Lord be praised for what he gives. And so begin."

## XVIII.

It was Monday afternoon, and the minister called at the Dell. "Ah, Mr. May," he said, "you are having a laugh here all to yourself. I heard it as I came past the window."

"O, I think it right to practise my host's laugh, as often as I can. I fancy it is good for my health, bodily and mentally."

"So Luther thought. For he said there was nothing the Devil hated worse than a good laugh."

"And I think so too," said Martin May.

"Man," the minister said, "man is the only creature that can laugh; and also he is the only creature that is beset by the Devil. So that it would seem as though laughter were a kind of weapon specially intended against the Devil; only that so often he gets it on his own side. No, no! Luther notwithstanding, I think it is doubtful whether the Devil has not more gain than loss by laughter. Hark, at the door of the public house! It is laughter inside. Hark in Parliament, that wise suggestion so modestly made! It is lost in shouts of laughter. Hark! what is it that is persuading that young man to turn round to the door of the gambling-house? It is a laugh of derision. And the virgin mind of yon maiden is being soiled, not with words so much as a laugh, — a sneering laugh."

"In what I was laughing at just now," said Martin May, "I am not sure but there is a sadness which ought to have kept me sober. I have been writing an answer to a letter from a man I hate. I hate him because he is a hypocrite, and makes a mask of the holy cause of freedom. He has written me a letter, in which he says, 'I have good reason to believe that you are a zealous, devoted friend of liberty everywhere. And therefore I have accepted the great honor of writing to you on behalf of the United Chartists and Friends of Humanity. I am empowered to invite you to address the United Chartists and Friends, on the earliest Friday evening that is convenient to you. You are one of those who are called to by downtrodden and oppressed human nature, weltering in the gore of centuries, and bruised by the infamous aristocracy. The unconquerable cause invites you. You come from the land of which Thomas Paine was a citizen and George Washington was President; and England expects you to do your duty.' Now I am a republican, and a zealous democrat. But this Fergus, I have seen him and heard him; and I know him to be an impostor. And I am not going to occupy the people with talking, while he picks their pockets."

"O, what an awful thing it is," said the minister, "that so much of the earnestness of this country should be under the misdirection of such men as this Fergus."

"I have been talking with a man of the name of Humphrey Sharples. Do you know him?"

"I know him. An unhappy man, wrong in body, mind, and estate; but in his mind worst of all! A man of fortitude and some fine capabilities; but, unfortunately for himself, a politician! At twenty years of age he was a strong, cheerful youth, singing and whistling at his field work. But a change came over him from attending a meeting of a Chartist club, one night. To be near the scene of political agitation, he sought employment in Manchester, and went there to live. And now he is the man you have seen him to be, from lodging in a dirty, smoky alley, — being only half employed, — attending political meetings night after night, often in rooms reeking with gin and tobacco, — fretting himself with his own wrongs, and the great wrongs of the country, — and reading unwholesome things, abusive newspapers, attacks on the institution of property, and false and true histories of royal, aristocratic, and clerical crimes. I believe he classes me among the oppressors, as though I were not even worse oppressed than himself. Poor man! There are millions like him, that only know they are tortured, but do not know how."

"You will excuse me, sir, I know, in my saying that I thought you had been quite absorbed in your books, schools, and preparations for the Sabbath. So that I did not think you had had much perception of the anomalies and wrongs here, which are so strange in my American eyes."

"Ah! I have long seen them. And indeed they have glared in my eyes painfully. Once I made a study of politics; and I grew fierce with it, and then wiser, and then sad. A large population crowded into a little island, and always growing denser, — everywhere twelve men struggling for the bread which is enough only for ten, — customs and institutions of the Middle Ages, blessings once, but which have lasted on so long in an altered world, as that now they only blight and curse, — taxation direct and indirect, — of all these things I know the effects, subtile often, and often more horrible than you would readily believe. I know of the underground channels by which the prosperity of poor men leaks away to feed what is so deep and broad and still, with woods and seats and grassy spots all round its margin, — the lake of abundance by yonder castle. When a strong, brave man, a farmer, struggles hard with a poor soil, a high rent, and tithe, and church-rate, and poor-rate, and fails and dies of a broken heart, — when men and women die unable to read the Bible, — when there cease living good, honest laborers, with whom a long lifetime of labor has never been sweetened with the least comfort, — there are groans go forth into the empty air. But also I know of the high quarter towards which those groans are turned and carried by the Angel of Justice."

The minister paused awhile and then continued: "But for me these are unwholesome thoughts. For so I have found them, with entertaining them. Yes, with these hot thoughts

I have found my eye for the beautiful fail me, — and my feelings all run to indignation and despair. And I found my soul dwindle in me, with the loss of the quiet that is her life. Were I ever so zealous and wise, yet in my position I could effect nothing whatever politically, either in the way of movement or instruction. And so, though I hold my own political opinions, yet I have turned away from that intense interest, which once drew me so absorbingly, and I try only to remember that I am a minister of Jesus Christ, who, though poor himself, could make many rich."

Martin May felt that in these words there was something of the history of the speaker's heart. And he looked earnestly at the minister, who continued, "What Humphrey Sharples suffers from poverty is nothing to what he suffers in other ways, — in having his sense of justice outraged, — in having his reverence fail for authority, — in having his feelings so embittered, as that almost he thinks and hopes all evil. In this manner, the wrong that is done him is worse than he knows, or ever will know in this world."

"It is terrible to think on the amount of mind which is vitiated in this country, and especially in the larger towns."

"Though perhaps in the great towns it is only that the universal mischief is more palpable. However, just hereabouts we are somewhat favored, and are exempt from some of the worst effects of Toryism. In this neighborhood, perhaps half of the farmers own the land which they cultivate, and so are independent of control. But there are wide tracts of country, over which there is not a farmer but votes with his landlord on all public matters, and not a farmer either, or indeed any one else, who dares to dissent from the Established Church. Against this oppression I am utterly powerless. And so I do not speak about it at all. I am silent on it, but not because I have been thoughtless on it always. For, Mr. May, I have not been so. But it is necessary for my people and my ministry that I possess my soul in peace, and not fret myself because of evil-doers. And also this sad condition of England is not evil deed altogether, for some and perhaps much of it is evil accident. And the rectification of it must be the work of time."

"And so it seems to me, sir."

"Here in England, Mr. May, before ancient oppressions can be made to cease in their effects, and before old neglects can be remedied, and deep, deep fountains of wrong can be closed up, slow, sure workmen must have had their time, and many, many years have passed away. But in the mean while, here are souls coming into the world, and needing to be sanctified on their way through it, — needing the ministry committed to my charge. Reform, reform! That is the cry all over the country. But time does not stop for reforms to be made. But in at the gate of birth souls keep coming, and across the world and out at the gate of death they keep going. And all the worse distracted is the time of their passage through, so much the more do they need the Gospel of Christ, and faithful words from some heart that is at peace with itself and in communion with God and Christ. And to this opinion of mine humbly I endeavor to conform my temper and my conduct. And that is the reason, Mr. May, why I am so unlike a fighting monk, or a bishop with a mace, or Pope Julian cased in armor underneath his vestments."

"Or Athanasius at Alexandria, struggling to maintain himself in his bishopric against Arius."

"Yes, or Athanasius. Here are souls which look to me for guidance, or which say they do. And I have got to direct them along ways which the political reformer may approach sometimes, and even cross, but which I cannot leave, so as to follow him to further him. These souls I have to watch; and I have perhaps to notice how on the mind of this old man there is a cloud thickening, — and how this young man is advanced within sight of a temptation, that beckons him, — and how this maiden is walking with her eyes on what is no trusty star, but a deceitful meteor, — and how this sufferer is beginning to despair, — and how this public event is likely to affect the minds of men, whether well or ill, whether to strengthen them in right feeling or weaken them. And so sometimes it may happen with a sermon of mine, that some hearer is guided safely past a danger which he never saw, — or some man has his courage called up against a trouble which he did not know was coming, — or some woman finds her heart grown unexpectedly strong against her next trial, — or some youth finds himself followed by earnest thoughts, that have come upon him he knows not how. To do something of this nature, and to keep myself and my little flock in the fellowship of the Holy Spirit, — this is my object, and I think it is my proper business; and I accept it as my calling."

"Do not rise, sir," said Martin May. "But must you really go, sir, so soon? It interests me much, to witness the state of English society, and to see how deeply it is marked with the effects of the past, — how the wholesome customs of the age of Alfred have become the grievances of the present day. And amid it all, for a man of much mind or heart, it must be a very difficult thing to keep patient."

"Yes. But still we should have to die, whether we were favored or aggrieved, — whether living under our old English institutions, or under such as you have in America, and which are renewed, it is said, every twenty years, like your wooden houses. Says St. Jerome, I think, to some correspondent, 'Do you not perceive how you have been a child, a boy, a robust youth, and how already you are now an old man? We die daily; we are changed every day. This moment of my writing is so much deducted from my life. We write; and then again we write in answer. Letters cross the sea, and ships plough the deep, and with every tide, every wave, our moments are diminished. We never can gain any thing but what we can appropriate to ourselves, through the love of Christ.' And that is my belief. And now I must return to my Parsonage."

## XIX.

Another evening Martin May sat on the bridge, and looked over into the shallow stream, and admired the beauty of the brook as it spread itself over the fine yellow sand for a bed. There came up the road two men. One of them was neatly dressed in black, and wore a white cravat. And the other, who led a calf in a string, was John Nock, a constable, living close by the Dell.

"Good evening," said Martin May. "That is a very pretty calf. What! Mr. Nock, have you been buying, or are you going to sell?"

"Sir, it is not my calf. It is Mr. Keeley's. At least, just now it is. I have nothing to do with it. I have only been doing my duty."

"It has been an unpleasant business," said Mr. Keeley. "But law is law. And so I told the old lady. And do not you think so, sir?"

"Certainly I do."

Mr. Keeley seemed much cheered, and said, "You see, sir, if you do not go by the law, what can you go by? That is what I say. And I am firm on it. And I went to that old lady and told her so, I should think five times. But it was all of no use. She would not pay, but only talk. And once she wanted to read to me; but I would not let her. She asked me into the parlor, and invited me to sit down; and so I thought certainly she was going to pay the rate. But not she! For she gets a great old book with Pennington on the back, and opens it and begins to read to me about a Hired Ministry. But I stopped her, and told her I was not the clergyman, but only the parish clerk. And would you believe it? This afternoon, when we took her the magistrate's order for payment, she wanted us to sit down and read a tract. As though a tract could be any thing against the magistrate's order!"

"And the order was for what?"

"For her to pay her church-rate, and the expenses of the summons and the hearing."

"And why would not she pay?"

"O, her conscience was her reason," she said. "But I said to her, 'If it is wrong in you to pay, it is worse in you to force us to make you pay twice as much as you ought. And so any way it would be better for you to pay the church-rate.' But not she, the old Quakeress! She would not."

"But then the Quakers do not go to your church. And so why should they pay to it?"

"Nor the Presbyterians, nor the Baptists, nor the Methodists. And they all pay, — they all pay. They all have to pay. For so the law is."

"And you Episcopalians, — do you pay to the Baptists or the Presbyterians?"

"Pay? No! For they cannot make us. They are not established. And that is just what I say. The law is the law, and the law makes the difference."

"O, then the Dissenters have to support the Established Church, and their own churches besides."

"Yes. The law lets them. Though they are not obliged to. For they could come to the Establishment, if they liked. But as I say, if the law is a bad law, let it be altered. But as long as the law is the law, why, let it be the law. You see, sir, that is plain enough. Yet that old Quakeress, I could not make her see it; though I said it over twenty times. And so she would not pay her rate, and we had to take the heifer."

"The church-rate is not tithe, is it?"

"O, no!" said the clerk, "it is nothing like tithe. It is not a quarter nor half a quarter as much."

"Now, for a farmer like Mr. Welby, what does tithe amount to, in the year?"

"About one hundred and twenty pounds. Well, now, there is Farmer Welby. He pays tithe to us, and church-rate, and never grumbles, — never. And yet he is a Presbyterian. And always at his house there is a jug of ale on the table when I call for the rate. But this old Quakeress, — she had a book on the table, and wanted to read to me; and would not pay. Though her rate is nearly nothing. And tithe she does not pay at all."

"That," remarked the constable quietly, "that is because the tithe has been redeemed on that field, years and years ago."

"Now let us be going," said the clerk. "But who is this galloping this way? It is Farmer Welby himself. I wish, Nock, we had not stayed here."

"How do you all do?" said Mr. Welby. "Mr. American, how do you do? You are getting fat. And I am glad to see it. For I did think once you had come here to die. Ah, it is beef makes the Englishman, and it would make an

Englishman of you, in a year. My cousin's beef ——"

"Will never make me your cousin's weight."

"O, I hope so, in time. But you do not want to be that yet, — not yet. But what have you got there, Mr. Keeley?"

"A calf, a heifer," said the clerk, doggedly.

"A heifer, a calf! Cannot I see it is a calf?" said Mr. Welby.

"Please, sir," said the constable, "we have been distraining for church-rate."

"Sorry for it, sorry for it! Pay the money, I say, and let us live in peace. Love and union and charity, — that is what I go for, Mr. May. And I wish we might all go for love and union and charity."

"Ah, if they were all like you!" said Mr. Keeley.

"Pretty calf! It wants its mother though! How it bleats, — poor little thing! And why would not the man pay?"

"Did not go to church."

"Nor do I. I go to chapel. It is hard, and I will not say but it is bad, that I should have to pay to a church I do not belong to, and do not believe in. But still, if I must pay, I will pay. And after all, my money might go in a worse way. But eh, man, what is the matter with you? Are not you well? But I say, whose calf was this, — what man's?"

"It was not any man's," said the clerk, and looked about for some way of escape.

"A woman's, then! It was not a woman's, though; was it? Do tell me, Mr. Keeley, it was not a woman's."

"It was, though," said the constable, pulling his hat over his eyes.

"And you took away a calf from a poor woman! You did, Isaac; did you? Then I say God have mercy on thee, Isaac Keeley. Take a poor woman's calf! Take it for the church, — a poor woman's calf!"

"She is not poor," said the clerk, fiercely.

"She is the Quaker lady at the Grange," said the constable.

The farmer grasped his horse by the mane, with both hands, and seemed as though swallowing his anger. At last he said calmly, "I would not have had this happen in the parish for five pounds, — no, nor for ten. She comes among us to live, without knowing any body, and without having one of her own people anywhere near. And she shows herself neighborly among us, and trusts herself and her daughter among us, as though she did not know what harm was. O, it was a beautiful sight, the way she came among us! And then such a quiet, kind, good woman!"

"I do not know that," sullenly objected the clerk.

"Why, Isaac, how can you stand there and say so? She gives away tons and tons of coal among the poor. She knits stockings and is always knitting for them. And only last week she gave John Hopperton a sovereign, because he had been ill for a month. And that is a kindness which the man told me of himself. From cottage to cottage, she going about in that neat little bonnet of hers, and doing so much good! And then that one of us should go and steal her calf from her! O, I cannot bear to think of it. I cannot bear it, Isaac! Love and union and charity, — where are they among us? Isaac, if you had come to me, I would have paid the money for her myself."

"She is old enough to pay for herself," muttered the clerk.

"A poor, lone woman," said Mr. Welby, "that has got no husband to see to her rights!"

"She has had her rights, and more than her rights, with my going to her house five or six times. But with all the trouble I took, she would not pay; but said she would testify against Babylon. And when I told her that she might do it, if she wished, and yet pay me the church-rate, as she ought; then she said that I was a dweller at Babylon, and a vessel in the temple. However, I should not have minded for that much. But she said she would give her testimony against me, and she called me the servant of a woman, and said that the woman was arrayed in purple and scarlet color. And when she said that, I told her that I knew what she meant, and that it was nothing to her how people dressed, and that scarlet was as good a color as drab, any time. There, now! That is what passed between us. And I have never told any body of it before. And I had not told you; had I, John Nock? And I say now, that because my wife wears a scarlet bonnet, it is no reason I should have it thrown in my face when I go to collect the church-rate. And so, the last time I was at the Grange, I determined the old lady should have the law in the same way that she would have it in any other parish. And I went to Justice Burleigh's, and got a summons for her. There, now! That was the way of it."

John Nock took off his hat with one hand, while he held the calf with the other; and he said, "Those Quakers are very peculiar people, as I have heard. And I do not think the old lady meant Keeley any harm by what she said, in calling him the servant of a scarlet woman. For while Keeley was in the cow-shed she said the same thing to me. And I have never had a wife, and do not mean to have either. Her saying that we came from Babylon, and calling us vessels in the temple of Mammon, and hirelings, and men after the manner of Achan, — with it all, I think she meant nothing, but only something of her religion."

"And now," said the farmer, "let us do what is right, if we can. Eh, moggy, moggy! Pretty calf! How it keeps smelling at me, as if it knew me! Does not it, pretty thing? Well, well, love and union and charity, — let us keep to that. And now, Isaac, man, if I have said any thing to offend you I will take it back, for I never meant it so. But at first I was vexed more than a little. And when I thought of the poor widow losing this calf, — God pardon me! — but I did not know whether to swear or cry; for I felt so like doing both. And now, Isaac, I will buy the calf, and we will send it back to its mother, poor thing; and let the old lady have it again."

"We cannot do that," said the constable. "For the calf cannot be sold by private contract. It has been taken by distraint; and so it will have to be sold by public auction in the market-place. For that is the law."

"Ah, well, soon it shall go back again. I remember, yesterday, I saw the lady leaning over the garden-wall. And on the side of the wall, in the pasture, was the young lady holding out her hand to this pretty calf. And the little thing nibbled at it; and then frisked, and ran away; and then came back, and then frisked again. And there stood the old cow close by, looking on, and enjoying to see the play of the sweet young lady and the pretty calf. And behind, there were those great old elm-trees, with the sun shining through them. It was a beautiful sight. And I stopped on the road to look at it. On market-day, then, we will send the calf back again. Love and union and charity! Do, neighbors, let us keep by that! And let us thank God that we know how."

## XX.

Percy Coke had come to Thorpe on a visit to his uncle, Mr. George Coke. He was calling on Mr. Lingard, and was conversing with him in his library.

Said the minister, " Nature is of religious use, not so much to show us God, as to justify our hearts to our understandings for believing in him."

Now this was an opinion which Percy Coke had himself arrived at, with long study, and much conversation with learned men, of many churches, and in several countries. And it was a conviction which he had thought might aid him in drawing for Christians the outline of a new form of theology. He suppressed his surprise at hearing uttered one of his own more private thoughts, and said, " That, — wherever did you obtain that thought ? "

The minister answered, "It came to me this morning, as I sat by the window thinking. And I suppose it is quite true. Because in nature we can discern only what we are prepared to see. And certainly, also, no man ever yet beheld God in earth or sky, by fixing his own time for the sight, or by going out of his house and saying, 'Now, like Adam, I will walk in the garden and hear God.' Communion with God, — it is not merely of the will or the intellect."

"A fine library you have," said Percy Coke. "And what a number of the old divines stand ranged upon these shelves! Shall I confess that I hardly know any thing of them? They stand here, your daily companions. Tell me, what is your opinion of them?"

"Yes, there they are, — Latimer, strong and homely, — and Taylor, strong and scholarly and poetical, — and South, making religion be witty, and wit be religious, — and Barrow, so trustworthy, — and John Smith, the accomplished, — and Henry More, the opposite of a materialist in every thing, — and Farrindon, who walks his way so sturdily, letting flash out suddenly the lamp of his genius in dark places. Yes, and there is Fuller there, dear Doctor Thomas, in whose eyes all innocent things laughed, and even vice looked ludicrous. And there is Tillotson, whom I have not looked at for many years, and Hall, and Bramhall, and Andrews, and Burroughs. And there is Cudworth, a mine to explore for learning, and a tower by which to ascend for wide speculation. And there is Burton, to read whose Anatomy of Melancholy Doctor Johnson once got up early. And next to him stands one who was no father of the Church, but only a son, — Sir Thomas Browne, a gentleman and a Christian, quiet and earnest and wise, laughing always, and always only in his heart."

"Go on, I beg you. For these are quite new to me; old as they are."

"O, those volumes are casuistical divinity. Those are lectures that were preached, week by week, at Cripplegate and other places in London, — discussions of cases of conscience."

"And what is this volume, with the label off, and which keeps clean with being used, while some of these casuists might perhaps be a little dusty, if they were stirred?"

"That is Catena Patrum, — a chain of the Fathers. And laying hold of that book reverently, I too am a link in the great golden chain that runs up the ages to Jesus Christ, — the succession of those by whose reverent acceptance the Divine word has been kept lasting on in the world, and speaking for a while Latin instead of Greek, and then the vernacular instead of Latin, and also from age to age adapting its arguments to the varying errors and the fresh perversities of the world."

"And here you have works of Aquinas, À Kempis, Augustine. These I should hardly have expected you would have read. Though why I should have thought so, I do not know."

"I count it essential to my office, to keep myself familiar with some of those old writers. I think I should be an unfaithful pastor, if I did not. For it is only through me that my congregation can be in any contact with the Fathers and the great Doctors of the Church. Farmer Welby on his lands, Abel Pratt behind the plough, John Johnson working at St. Crispin's trade, — it is only through me that there can come on to them, reach them, some of the better influences of antiquity. My congregation, — it is through me that they are to be kept in correspondence with the Past, — the great, earnest, wise, meditative Past."

"Right, sir, right. And it is by men like you that society is kept from degenerating. For how quickly they are forgotten, — the footsteps of the noblest, even in places that were once their familiar walk! And how soon they perish, the words of the wise, if there be no wise man to keep repeating them. Lately, where the gentle, thoughtful Evelyn dwelt I have walked about, but I never heard there one word that was like a trace of him. And at Twickenham there is nothing survives of Pope in the minds of the inhabitants, except his name and fame, which are talked of in a way ——"

"Yes, sir. But there are some of the aphorisms of Pope that are common proverbs now. You have not heard my housekeeper talk, I think. Her conversation is almost a string of proverbs. And they are traceable, I have no doubt, some of them to Pope, and some to Shakspeare, and some to Chaucer, and some to wits among the preaching friars, and some, I am certain, to Danish settlers and Norman conquerors. And if you will notice, you will find that of the peasantry, especially the shrewder portion, a great part of their speech is of the character of proverbs, — old sayings, — phrases caught by the son from the father.

"Is it so? Then the Past does live on in them, of itself."

"The vulgar Past does. No! That is a

word of too much depreciation. But it is so, that, for the most part, those old proverbs are the shrewd utterances of the natural man, not the spiritual, — things such as Dick says to Jack, and which Jack agrees stand to reason."

"That," said Percy Coke, "that is as I should expect. Just as there are countries in which all the people would pick up glass beads, and leave lying on the ground pearls of great price."

"Men of work, worldly effort and worldly struggle, — to them, talking together, the readiest and the safest things to say are maxims of worldly prudence, worldly criticism, worldly comfort. And it is as we see. The shrewdness of the past gets perpetuated in the world, so much more easily, and indeed so much more surely, than the devoutness of it, or the humility, or the faith."

"That is worth thinking of. And it makes one feel the necessity there is for the Christian Church, as an organization conducive to civilization. And I have been thinking that it is a great thing, — notable, and indeed sublime, — the existence in a small town of a library like this, with you in it, as the mouthpiece of ages and nations, poets, philosophers, and divines."

"Through me Chrysostom still making his voice heard, and Augustine uttering now and then some of his better sayings,—those words of a man so wise in the struggles of the soul."

"Yes, and I fancy that they speak in your voice with less alloy of error than when they preached with their own lips. But indeed it is a wonderful thing to think of, for the manner in which it has come to pass, and in itself it is a great thing, that these farmers and artisans and laborers—men indigenous to these acres—should have for their friend and counsellor a man who is the intimate acquaintance of Augustine, and the friend of Aquinas, and the companion of Jeremy Taylor, and the fellow-worshipper of George Herbert."

"In that Temple of which the width is what only God knows, though known to every body is its chief corner-stone, Jesus Christ," said the minister.

"Well said. And here,—a German edition,—here you have Plato."

"Whom you are better able to describe than I am, I do not doubt."

"I was going to ask you," said Percy Coke, "what you think is the reason of the difference between the forms into which ancient and modern writers put their thoughts. With the moderns, the utterance of philosophy is a monologue.

But with the ancients it was not so. Even Plato does not sit down by himself and soliloquize. But up the heights of philosophy, by paths of his own discovery, he takes his friends. And on some lofty summit he and they sit down together, and, breathing the pure of heaven, they discourse together on the subject of the world below, — the fools in it, and how men may become wise, — on life, its mystery and tendencies, — on the horrible character of a people spoiled by lawlessness and the sophists, — on the soul, and the divine light which comes with it into the world, a light though so soon altered from the divine to the devilish by being fed with the oil of sensuality. The writings of Plato are almost only dialogues."

"And of our earlier modern literature there was much which assumed a dramatic form. Of the Scriptures you know what is the literary texture. But as to your question, I cannot answer. But I suppose the answer to it is in the dogmatic character which has come over philosophy from the sectarianism of our times, and perhaps in a confidence of opinion, which is willing to shun as unnecessary the little room for uncertainty left open between the persons of two speakers."

"That last is the real reason, I think," said Percy Coke. "I do not know why; but to-day it does strike me as something great and remarkable, the existence of this library in a place like this Thorpe. O these books, so many and in so many languages! Only to be amongst them is a something of responsibility. These authors, one in a voice from afar off like a waterfall, — another in the low, gentle murmur of sorrow, — another in the decisive, solemn tones of a judge, — and another in the sweet, musical words of a poet, — all these authors, hundreds of them, calling to the conscientious student, 'Let me be heard,' —— "

"And along with them, though of a diviner sound and another origin than they, and more rightful in its solicitations, the Word that is the same yesterday, to-day, and for ever."

"And then there are the historians of it, and the translators of it, and the commentators on it. For many men it must be a great temptation and a welcome belief, — the fancy which has its zealous advocates just now, — that in the soul there is an intuitive and spontaneous perception of all spiritual truth."

"The first five years of my ministry I preached with great satisfaction to myself and my people.

Yet all the while I was preaching the doctrine of Confucius, and not the Gospel of our Lord and Saviour Jesus Christ. I preached to the souls of men, without myself being conscious of a soul, — a soul convinced of sin, sensible of the world's mystery, wretched with its own helplessness, and open to the Holy Spirit."

"How do you mean that you once preached the doctrine of Confucius?"

"I preached morals, excellent morals, and thought they were Christianity. And they are not the whole of Christianity, nor indeed what is most peculiar in it. Have you ever read the Moral Sentences of Confucius? Because, if you have, you must know that there are some persons whose Christianity is indeed older than Christ."

"No, I have not seen them. But I should have thought that into your present opinions your mind had unfolded gradually, and from your youth upwards."

"No," said the minister, "no! More truly than so, by my mental history, I am a man of this age, — this age so woful for the deep, earnest thinker, — this age, when of all institutions and principles the foundations seem loosened from beneath, and when there come, blown in upon us to darken and blight us, heavy fogs of unbelief, from that wide, sullen ocean that rolls in upon the island of our human existence,—the ocean of nothingness, and death, and ignorance."

Here Percy Coke turned to the window, and tears started to his eyes. The minister thought he was merely looking into the garden; and so finished what he was saying: "Strange time! when everywhere there is contention for the Gospel, and so little knowledge of it! But I, here,—I strive to be, not of the time nor of the world, but of the Church. As a Christian I have other, greater helps, which I find real and effective. But yet, sitting in meditation in this room, there reach me from the great ages of the past lights not feeble, and helpful voices my heart leaps at. Yes, whatever else be true or false,—my struggles now over, and my misgivings and doubts all over now,—I am conscious of Christ in my heart, the hope of glory. And by the lights that gleam up the ages, I see distinctly to Calvary, and into the awful darkness, and on the cross, and on to the death that is life."

Here Percy Coke turned from the window in some little agitation, and rather suddenly took his leave.

## XXI.

On the Friday morning after the talk on the bridge, Martin May went into Thorpe. It was market-day; and all round the old cross were rows of booths, at which were sold butter and eggs, and ducks and chickens, vegetables, and meat, and confectionery. And at one end of the square were pens full of pigs, sheep, and oxen. Nearly all the ladies of Thorpe were out in the market, buying their weekly stock of provisions for the larder. It was a busy, lively, pleasant scene.

At the entrance of the market a man was selling pins, made by machinery, as all pins are now. And in a loud voice he sang some doggerel verses on the uses and excellence of his pins. But he was utterly ignorant of there being in existence an old act of Parliament of the reign of Henry the Eighth, according to which no person ought to offer for sale any other pins than what are double-headed, and have the heads soldered fast to the shank, and are well smoothed, and have the shank well shaven, and the point well filed and sharpened.

Not far from the man with the pins, and close by the whipping-post, with nobody near him, a blind man led by a dog in a string was singing the ballad of Lord Bateman's Daughter. And as the vender of the pins did not know that he was selling what was contrary to the law, so this blind beggar, by wearing a red cap, did not know that he was complying with a law enacted in the reign of Queen Elizabeth, and according to which on Sabbaths and holidays every person above the age of seven years ought to wear a cap of wool, knit and dressed in England.

Among all the persons in the market, the most conspicuous was the bellman, — a short man, and very corpulent. He was a person of many offices. He was a constable, a beadle at St. John's Church, a clerk in a court of law, a head-borough or inspector of weights and measures, and bellman or town-crier. He was dressed in scarlet breeches, a scarlet waistcoat, and a plush-colored coat richly ornamented with gilt lace. And he wore a three-cornered hat. In his hand he held a tall, thick staff, surmounted by a gilt bell. From his pompous look and slow movements it might have been thought that in him were embodied all the law and magistracy of the whole county. And yet he was only the bellman of Thorpe.

Exactly as the church clock struck twelve an auctioneer mounted the steps of the cross, and sold the calf which had been distrained from Grace Thoroughgood for the church-rate. It was bought by Farmer Welby, and was immediately returned to the Grange.

Close by the church gates there was an exhibition of Punch and Judy. In appearance it was something like a clock-case, with puppets playing in a little chamber at the top. Inside the case stood the man, who made the figures move and talk. Around this exhibition there was a crowd assembled, rejoicing in Punch for his immoral opinions, his wit and lawlessness, and especially for his wicked treatment of the constable, who came to arrest him for his conduct towards his wife. Exactly opposite this show Martin May met the bellman, who was red in the face, and held out at arm's length his tall staff with the gilt head.

"A very improper concern to be allowed, this

is," said the bellman, "because it is calculated to draw the authorities into contempt. And in my opinion it ought to be brought under the Act for the Suppression of Vagrants. I do not know what your opinion is, but that is mine, sir."

"Well, myself," said Martin May, "I think any thing is wrong which abates respect for righteous authorities properly constituted."

"You are a very sensible man, Mr. May. But these fools here laughing at dolls —— "

"Dolls, sir!" said Martin May, in a tone of surprise. "Dolls do you call them, those semblances of man?"

"Why, you do not think them any thing else!"

"Dolls, sir! To me they are typical of human nature, and representative of the problem of existence in its development."

"I am no scholar; but what I do know is, that there is a man inside the curtain."

"Are you sure? Have you ever seen him come out? For I never have. And I have often watched for him."

The bellman was a superstitious man, and believed in ghosts, and magic, and witchcraft. And, deceived by the gravity of Martin May, he began almost to fancy that the exhibition was not a mere affair of vagrants.

Martin May continued, "I know it is the common opinion that they are merely puppets to laugh at. But I do not laugh at them, for I can see that there belongs to them that by which they are some little akin to men and women. You see they act and talk."

"But is not it because they are made to," asked the bellman, his dignity collapsing in him.

"And has it never occurred to you, that there is a power behind you, which walks you about and makes you talk?"

"You mean the magistrates?"

"No, I mean a power that is aback of the magistrates as well as yourself."

"Ah, then, that must be the lord-lieutenant of the county," said the bellman, beginning to recover from his bewilderment.

"Something like it. That warrant you showed me down at the Dell ——"

"I have served it, and the man is fast in prison."

"And at the beginning of the warrant was it not said that the man was instigated by the Devil?"

"Yes, always that is what it begins with."

"And among all these people here, do not you think there are instigations good and bad, that move one man one way, and another man another, making them feel and talk and act and be just like these puppets? Well, it is so. Now on this account there are persons who believe in the doctrines of pantheism. But myself I do not. Though I agree with Sir Thomas Browne, who says he is sure there is a common spirit that plays within us, and yet makes no part of us."

Again the man of office was bewildered. Yet from the sound of the last two or three words he thought there had been something said which he ought to understand. At last he said, in a tone of concession, "May be so. Though any thing that sounds like that I have never heard before out of church."

"And of course it is what we all understand and believe while we are in the church. But this exhibition here, — I think its metaphysical usefulness is very great. And on reflection, sir, you must yourself perceive it, I am sure."

The bellman looked flattered, and his glance at Punch was less ferocious.

"Are you aware," Martin May asked, "that the beginning of this exhibition was with the mysteries, the moralities, which were a kind of play that used to be acted in the churches?"

"Ah," said the bellman in a tone of triumph,

"that must have been in the times of ignorance, when the Papists had the churches, and did in them any thing they liked. For I have been told by the clerk, that just inside the door of this very church, in the hole in the wall, there used to be water for the people to dip their hands in. Any thing they liked, those Papists used to do in church."

"Well," said Martin May, "and now what do you do in church?"

"Do! Why, do not you know, sir? Do not you come to church? Do! We do nothing."

"Do not you think their brains are like strings that are played on,—these people's?"

"These poor people's? O, yes, and nothing better."

"Like strings in a harp, some stretched to one note, and some to another. And there sweeps among them some invisible breath of life, and makes them thrill with thought and feeling and incitement to action. So that, when you with a warrant in your hand arrest a man who has been instigated by the Devil, it is really the plastic spirit of the universe turning in upon itself. And you are not yourself, though you think you are; and the criminal is not himself either."

"Well," said the bellman in a tone of apology, "I must confess I was not quite myself that day. But though you noticed it, I hope you will not speak of it. But that man, sir, that criminal, was a desperate character, as I knew, and so I thought to strengthen myself against him by calling at the Hare and Hounds. You know the house, sir: a very respectable house. And Sir Thomas Browne I have great respect for. He is a justice of the quorum. He does not often attend the monthly meeting of the magistrates, because it is so far from Browne Castle to Thorpe. But when he is present, it is a great satisfaction to us officers."

"We do understand one another," said Martin May.

"I hope so, sir," said the bellman cheerfully.

"I am sure so, for myself. Good morning!"

Martin May went in at the churchyard gate, and seated himself upon a tomb. After a little time of meditation he said to himself, "With Punch to look at, and that bellman to talk with, I have come to understand that pantheistic philosophy, I think. It is the philosophy of a head that has never had rise up to it one thought from out of the heart. It is the delusion of a man of no heart, no hand, no purpose. A pantheist weeping at a grave would be an absurdity. When it can be, it is well that the dead should be among us. With the dead beneath our feet, and the sun overhead, and in our ears the sound of people close by, who labor and suffer, and love and sorrow, and who are earnest with things hard to bear, or painful to obtain, or liable to be lost, — in a place like this, in this place of the dead with the living about, — one cannot do otherwise than believe in God, that he is God. And yet we might be no more than puppets, were we to be judged of by the manner in which some men are wrought upon by prejudices, suspicions, fears, sorrows, and ambition. A right feeling about life, and what it is in God's eye, — a man cannot have it form in his mind by the mere ingenuity of logic. He can hope for it reasonably only by keeping on the ways of nature, and by living a life of labor and rest, conversation, and joy and sorrow, and prayer, — by letting every emotion of his heart have its proper expression, and yield its proportionate influence to the temper of his soul, and so to his manner of judgment. Not puppets, not animated dust, are we, but souls, living souls! We are souls God has made for his own joy, — creatures for his Godhead to circle in its arms, and to brood over with its fatherly love. Our prayers, — he may know that they are coming, yet he loves to have them come up to him. In our ignorance, not that we can honor him or help him! But he loves to feel us groping after him, even though blindly, as well as in the dark."

## XXII.

Towards the end of September, John West had come from Manchester to Thorpe, on a visit to the Dell for a day. In conversation Martin May said, "Do you know Mr. Coke? I think I have heard his name, as that of a public man in Manchester."

"Yes, and the terror of the Tories."

"Indeed!"

"Yes. And by a high authority he has been pronounced the most effective orator of the day, if not the most eloquent. O, they are wonderful, — his power of sarcasm, his accurate knowledge, his presence of mind, and sometimes his vehemence, and at other times his imperturbable calmness! There have been few men who have stood forth more bravely than he against oppression, and in behalf of the poor."

"You confirm the impression I had taken of him from conversing with him."

"I have seen conceited men address him, and with only speaking to him evidently they have felt themselves confuted. On some public occasion I have known him be surrounded by opponents and the shouts of an angry mob. And amid it all he stood calm and confident. And then, almost without his speaking a word, there receded from about him all opposition; just as the sea subsides of itself from about a rock, and leaves it standing firm, and apparently even higher than before. But the minister, — I hope you understand him; for if you do, you must admire him."

"I admire him very much. And I owe him much for the good he has done me. His influence over me is very great. And yet how it is exerted I hardly know. Often and often he says things, from which I could almost suppose that he had looked into my mind, and seen what was wanting there. Sometimes, in conversation, he leads me away to topics corrective of my morbid feelings. And I become aware of what he has done with me only when I find myself high up above the gloomy mists, with wholesome air about me and the bright heavens overhead. And how finely he talks, does not he? Such a noble, solemn strain of thought as there is in his conversation sometimes! And such a wide acquaintance, West, as he has with old writers!"

"Yes, May. But have you noticed how he uses them? Though I have no doubt that he does not know himself. He seldom quotes from an author for the purpose of sustaining himself in an argument. But when he is uneasy at the turn which conversation is taking, or when himself he feels dull, then he quotes some old poet or divine. But he does dearly love an old book. Last summer, on his way to dine with a friend, he lost more than an hour by happening on horseback to take out of his pocket a volume which he had never read. He read in it page after page, till the horse stopped with him at a door five miles away from the house he was going to. I suppose all the while that he must have had some unconscious care of the horse; for he is a good horseman, and can take a leap like a huntsman almost."

"But a man of his character and situation and domestic tastes,—how is it that he has never been married."

"Well for him that he has not been, perhaps. Years ago he was engaged to a lady. So it is said."

"Was he, indeed? Who was she?"

"You know her, I think. At least you have seen her, — Miss Barbara Shelmerdine."

"What! That duchess! A woman that is a lady evidently, and a very superior lady, and yet perhaps some little — possibly some very, very little of a shrew."

"The same. Though I do not believe, and indeed I feel quite sure, that there never was an engagement between the minister and her."

"Ah, well, supposing there was once, then how was it broken off?"

"But there never was any engagement between them of a matrimonial nature, I believe. And so it is not worth while telling what people say was the manner of its being broken. But I will tell you what I do know to be true. I was told it by the poor woman concerned in it. And I think perhaps she has never told any one else. One day the minister called upon her at her house. And on opening the parlor door, he saw and heard Miss Shelmerdine in a passion with a poor dressmaker, who stood at her table pale and crying. It is possible that the minister may have caught a word or a look of the lady's excitement. The presence of a lady like her in a rage, — what a situation for him to be in, was not it? And then that the poor dressmaker should be standing there, and needing some word in her behalf! Just a word or two the minister said, and then drew back from his unlucky entrance. 'The ornament of a meek and quiet spirit! See in yonder glass what a loss it is!' Cannot you conceive of how he said it in that odd tone which he has at times, half roguish, half sorrowful?"

"What an unfortunate occurrence! But the lady was at the chapel last Sunday."

"And always attends there very regularly, when she is in Thorpe."

"But is she of that violent temper still, do you think?"

"No; I do not think she is so at all. Indeed, I think very highly of her, as a lady of many accomplishments, much benevolence, and great energy. And she is very cheerful and very religious."

"But then what an incident in her life for the minister to witness! How could one ever forget such a sight? But religious, beneficent, cheerful, energetic, accomplished! That is a noble character. And yet what a discord with it your anecdote makes!"

"Yes," said John West, "it is in the finest strain of music that a momentary jar sounds the worst."

"And," said Martin May, "all the more wise and good and beautiful is the character of any person, so much the more repulsive sounds one foolish word from him, or an improper utterance, or one incorrect speech; and yet perhaps it may have been elicited from him in some moment of nervous irritation, or wayward feeling, or hasty, bewildered thought. Sometimes we dislike a person for an action all the more, the more unlike him we feel it is. But surely this is not reasonable."

## XXIII.

While the minister was at his breakfast, Mrs. Satterthwaite stood by the door of the study, and said, "If you please, sir, I have finished what you told me to do last night. They say that every potter praises his own pot, and the more if it be broken. Yet I think I have done it well, though I say it that should not say it. And sir, it is like the old saying, that my cow gives a good mess of milk and then kicks it down; for all the pears are blown down off the tree at the corner."

"Are they ripe, — quite ripe? Then you may divide them among the children in the school. Though it will be better to let the teacher distribute them."

"It is an ill wind that blows nobody good; and last night it was a good wind for the children. And, sir, I have been to see that woman that came here to beg. And it is quite true, what I told you. And it makes it true, what I said, — all saint outside, and devil within."

"What! Is she so thoroughly bad?"

"She tried to excuse herself. But I told her that crows are never the whiter for washing. When she saw that I had found her out, then she pretended to cry. However, I let her know that I was not so cunning but I knew what weather it was when it rained. But then, sir, she has been badly brought up; and so she really is excusable a little. And so it might be proper, perhaps, to allow her something out of the poor's money, because, as they say, one might as well be out of the world as be beloved by nobody in it. But then a person may buy gold too dear. And to lick honey from thorns is to pay too dear for it. But then, again, we are all Adam's children, though silk makes a difference. But the woman is not worse than old Sally, and perhaps is not as bad. And that shows, again, that one man may steal a horse while another must not look over the hedge."

"But, Mrs. Satterthwaite, you cannot mean that old Sally has ever been a horse-stealer?"

"O, no, sir! no, sir! And there now! That shows how true the old saying is, that wit is folly, unless a wise man has the keeping of it. And sir, last evening, while you were out, Mr. West called with Mr. May."

"John West? And how was he?"

"O, sir, quite well. Merry and wise, — that is what he is. Once, a long while ago, when he was a boy, and his father had set him to do some work which he did not like, I said to him, that care killed a cat, but there was no living without it. And so now when he sees me he says to me always, that there is no living without what killed the cat. A fool may chance to put something into a wise man's head. And that is what I put into his."

"He is prospering at Manchester."

"O, yes, he is making hay now while the sun shines. And he can, because at the beginning he was willing to cut his coat according to his cloth, and to plough with such oxen as he had."

"Yes," said the minister, "when John West was a youth, he was very promising. And now it is very delightful to see what an excellent man he is."

"Sir; an idle brain is the Devil's workshop. And when Mr. John was a boy he never kept it. Always he had his wits about him, and could tell that forecast is better than hard work. And so now he is a gentleman, because of his believing that where there is a will there is a way, and that if you would be Pope you must think of nothing else."

"And how was Mr. May? He has been away from the Dell for a week, has not he, Mrs. Satterthwaite?"

"Yes, sir. He and Mr. John, — they are hand and glove. He says now he gets to be as hungry as a church mouse. Though I know once at his food he was as nice as a nun's hen. But he knows now that hunger is the best sauce, and that medicines are not meant to live on. And so he will soon find that health is better than wealth."

"I am glad to hear that still he is improving in health."

"And, sir, there is come to Mr. Robert Gentle's the lady that was on a visit there, and was ill, five or six years ago, — Miss Lawton. She is a cousin of the Gentles. You must remember her, certainly. A very beautiful lady she used to be, and very lively. And she used to talk very sweetly, though sometimes very seriously. Poor woman! By her look I do not think she has been happy. For now she seems so timid, and like one who had been expecting bad news for a long time. What it is I do not know. But I am sure,—poor, dear woman, —that her heart knoweth its own bitterness."

## XXIV.

There was a summer-house at the end of the garden, behind Mrs. Gentle's house. And in it, one warm afternoon of October, sat Mr. George Coke and Louisa Lawton.

"And you do not despise me, you do not think it was wrong in me," said the lady, "that I wrote that letter to you?"

"No, no! How could I? For do not I know you? Never for a moment has there been a word or action of yours that I have misunderstood. The honor, the tenderness, the purity, the generosity, the humility, the religiousness of your nature, — do not I know them all like the familiar strings of a harp? And whenever there sweeps through them some breath of resolution, do not I know — and even if I could not feel, yet must not I know and be sure — how heavenly the music that is made? Ah, no! Whatever you have been moved to speak, — always it has been to me what I have been humbled with, for it has been so good. And yet also it has been so kind, that always with thinking of it all my soul has flowed toward you in confidence."

As though she had not heeded these words, the lady added quickly, "But whether or not it humbled me in your eyes, I felt that it was due to you from me that I should write as I did. Though perhaps it was through my affection that I felt so. And if it has been so, George, you will allow for it. For though my troth was given back, yet my heart was not; and always it has been with you. O that ill day, when there came to me that sad message from you! I was grieved with it, and angry, and mortified. For it seemed to say to me, 'Forsake me, like every one else, for I am sure you must wish it.' And then, when I thought upon it, I did not know how to understand it. I could not tell what to think, — whether you distrusted my being faithful to you in adversity, or whether you wished to be just, and not hold me to a companionship in poverty, or whether you wished to be free, and not have my weight on your arm, while struggling up the world again. And then, after a time, with thinking it all over so much, I became ill."

"My poor Louisa!"

"And when I recovered, I thought then it was too late for me to seek an explanation as to your message, through my dear father. Afterwards I hoped that in some way, by some occurrence, some accident, there might arise some mutual understanding between us. And then my dear father fell ill, and needed all my care, and all the love I could show him. My poor father! But with minding him I grew calm again, and almost cheerful. With praying for him every night and morning, and thinking what things would soothe him, and reading to him, and watching him from hour to hour, time went on with me, — days, months, and years. And the more helplessly dependent on me my father became, the more strongly there arose in me the feeling of a daughter to sustain him. And with his dear smile on me all day, and his blessing me every night, O, so tenderly and solemnly, I felt life brighten about me, and keep bright, as though with the yellow, pensive light of one of those days that summer ends with, and which you used to love much. And yet often, not far off, it seemed to me as though there were a dark cloud, in the shadow of which you stood alone and looked at me. And sometimes I wondered that you never approached nearer. Yet I was glad and grateful that you did not. Because my father I never could have left. Nor could I ever have borne to have heard you calling to me."

"Yes, it has all been for the best, Louisa, — all for the best. Till the last three or four years, I was very poor both in money and prospects. And mere poverty, — I could not have asked you to love that. And that was all I was then."

"No, do not say so, George; do not say so. For at least always you were yourself, — your fine, noble, generous self."

"Ah, no, Louisa, no!" said Mr. Coke. "No companion for your holy cheerfulness should I have been latterly! And indeed I should have been unworthy of your sweet sympathies."

"O, no! do not say so. Though it has not been what we had hoped, — our lot in life."

"We are free to walk hither and thither on the field of existence; yet there is on us a divine constraint, that is invisible and unfelt, but which guides us in the direction of its own ends. And are there not some positions, into which we feel sure that we have been divinely brought? Sternly we may have been guided into them, but if divinely too, then cannot we wait in them, rest in them, patiently, expectantly, our hands clasped, and our eyes on God?"

"So right-minded, so pious, you have always been, George. It was not for any fault, for any error in you, that our two lives have been so ——"

"Hush, Louisa, hush! It is not of me you should speak so. For I have known what it was to turn from God and despair. Yes, and I have looked at God, and held as nothing — a risk for chance, a tiresome trouble — this gift of his, — this divine gift of life."

"And your despair, I have been some cause of it. O, if only I had ——"

"Your companionship would have been too great a happiness for me, with God looking on, — unmerited happiness, which almost I might have been afraid of enjoying in his eye, — the Holy One. Too great a good for me, — yes, indeed, Louisa, you would have been too good for me, as you remember I always used to say you would."

"But always I felt it could not be so, because myself I was not worthy of the sunshine of your eye; and because I was not of a spirit great enough to give you back thoughts for your great thoughts, and words that should be a fair exchange for your noble, stirring, joyous words. Ah, if only it had happened that your betrothed had been some braver, better woman than myself, what is there you might not have become! — a prince among merchants, — a statesman with millions to admire and love and honor you. All this you might have been, and would have been, but for me. Very useful you have been and very widely; but I know well that you would have been known of, all over the world, but for my fault, my failing you in your time of trouble, and so weakening your courage. But indeed, indeed, at that time, miserably bewildered, I did not know what to think. But now I know what I ought to have done. But I did not do it. And it was because my heart was not worthy of you."

"If it is mine still, Louisa, do not speak so of it. And it is mine, I know, and always has been."

"Yes," said the lady, "always it has been. And so it was all the worse in me that I did not see what I ought to have done on receiving the news of your misfortune, and the message by my father absolving me from my engagement. And then, too, often and often I have sat still in an evening, and been pleased with fancying, that, notwithstanding our broken engagement, still you were surely mine, — moving about in the world, and standing on some of its high places, and thinking of me all the while. Indeed, George, it was wrong in me to please myself with believing that you were mine, and yet not to have let you know that I held it nothing, — that message from you, setting me free from our engagement."

"Hush! Do not accuse yourself so. As to our present positions, do not let me hear from you one word of self-accusation. I should not be worthy to listen to it, even were it true, which it is not. You will not think that, for you are so good, and you will not believe it; yet it is so. And in what separates us now, it is I that am to blame, and more sadly than I can tell you."

"Your pride, — that is what you are thinking of. For, George, you are a very proud man, and you always were, — proud of your character, which you ought not to be, — and proud of holding yourself independent of every body, which is a thing you ought not to wish to do. You will pardon my speaking so, George, will you not?"

13

"Say on, Louisa. You are right, and you can say nothing but what is right. I have been proud, very proud, wickedly proud."

"No, not so, not wickedly, not blamably." Here the lady blushed all up her face, and under her ringlets of hair. "But, George, why should that pride of yours hinder what I do believe would be your happiness? And why should it blight my life? You have my heart. O, do not hold it cruelly, and have it wither with your pride."

"I, Louisa, I! Never!"

"O, if only you knew, in writing that letter, how I struggled with maidenly modesty!"

"I do know it. In my mind's eye I have seen you writing it. I have seen it all, — the blush that came and went upon your face, even when you were alone, — resolution in your mind, wavering with modesty, but sustained by womanly generosity, — and affection from long years, rolling in upon you in a flood of pure, urgent emotion."

"Why, then, George, why may we not hope, — have those dear sweet hopes of long ago revive? But I know how you are thinking that you are not now what you were once. But believe me, that what a true woman needs most in the object of her affections is not comfort for herself, but a something for her to comfort, — not an arm that can surround her with pleasures, but a name she can honor, and an eye she can look to, for the loving way of its watching her. Something to think of, to toil for, to fear for, to suffer for, — something she might proudly die for, — this is what a woman needs more truly than a servant to attend her, or a luxurious home to dwell in."

Here over the countenance of Mr. Coke there went an expression of anguish. And he bowed his face on his hands. The lady, while speaking, had turned her eyes from him, and so she had not noticed his agony. And she continued. "Almost now I am rich. And in some warm climate, with me about you always, to watch, and tend, and love you, soon you would recover your health, and return again to England, and be what you ought to be, — the admiration of the people, and mine, my own, all the while. For with rest, and care, and a visit to a warmer climate, you would recover quite certainly. So Doctor Blinkhorn says."

"He!" said Mr. Coke, in a tone strangely expressive of pain and anger and tenderness. "And he has caused you this further trial, my poor, dear Louisa! Blinkhorn with his ignorance! O, indeed, Louisa, it is not as he tells you! God's will be done! And for me that will is my death. I must indeed die soon; so my London physician tells me. Your love sweetens for me my life at the end. But it cannot do more. But see. There is Mrs. Gentle opening the gate, and she is coming to remind me that it is time I should go into the house. I will go and meet her. And, Louisa, do you come after me."

## XXV.

Mr. Coke had resolved to retire from business, and desired to have his nephew Percy succeed to him. And Percy had told him of his history for five years previous, and of his purposes and hopes as to the future.

"And you think they are new, — your positions in theology," said Mr. Coke. "But I must tell you that I do not think they are, even here in England. I think you would find them known to our minister here, if you were to talk with him."

"I must confess, sir, that I have been surprised at some thoughts I have heard him express."

"I do not wonder at your surprise. For almost there is a whole literature in existence, which yet has never been heard at Oxford. And even if you do not know it, you can easily suppose it. For you, who have refused to subscribe the Thirty-Nine Articles, and who have thereby pulled to the door in your own face, — the door by which Oxford lets a man out on the field of public life, — even with you the first impulse on taking up a book is to ascertain, if you can, whether or not the author is of Oxford or Cambridge. I tell you, that there are men who have been educated in theology, as a science, and who have traversed in all freedom the wide field of religious speculation, and explored the deep mines of patristical learning, and who have built themselves up in lofty convictions of their own. And of the very existence of these men there is no knowledge at Oxford. And so much the worse for Oxford! And you yourself have studied for years in Oxford, and journeyed from one foreign university to another, and meditated in seclusion, year after year, only to arrive at last at positions which are very similar to the principles which our friend has held for several years. What bewilderment and trouble you would have been saved by an hour's talk four years ago! Only I suppose, even four years ago, your Oxford vanity would not have endured a Presbyterian minister. You remember the last time you called on me. You opened a book which lay on the table, and which I had just had handsomely bound. And when you saw it was the Life of George Washington, you shut it suddenly, and muttered something about a demagogue. But whether the epithet was meant for me or Washington, or both, I did not know."

"I remember the silly action. But I did not think you had heard me. And now, if it is not too late, sir, I ask your forgiveness for my folly."

"Your folly, — yours! It was not yours, Percy, but your cap's, — your Oxford cap's! For there are certain important subjects on which a man thinks, one way or another, according as he wears the crown of a monarch, the coronet of a peer, a student's cap tufted or a commoner's, the shovel-hat of a vicar, the fur cap of a grenadier, the broad-brimmed hat of a Friend, or the cheap felt of a peasant. It is so with nine hundred and ninety-nine men out of a thousand. But you yourself are the one man in a thousand. And now I have forgiven you, have not I? And so then, Percy, you persist in declining to succeed me in business?"

"Yes, sir, I am not fit for the place, nor would it suit me."

"And why not? Will you tell me why you cannot deal in calicoes and live, instead of starving as an usher in a school, with the hope some time of starving to death, as a man of genius? Your reasons now, — come, tell me. You have none? Then what have you?"

"Feelings, persuasions from within, aspirations, a sense of ——"

"Sense? Nonsense."

"Did not I tell you, uncle, that I had nothing to answer which you would accept as a reason?"

"Percy, you are twenty-eight years of age. And yet, because you are an honest student, you can have no prospect of success in the world. All over the kingdom, in every church, the pulpit-door is shut against you, and so is the door of every grammar-school in which you might hope to be a master. However, you are a man not only of Latin and Greek, but also of the commercial languages, French, German, and Dutch, — you are a man of perseverance and industry, — and address and character, — a man of twenty times as much mathematics as will keep a leger, — and with a memory that will hold any day all the prices, the news, and the sales of the Exchange, — a man whom any body would trust for your looks! And you will not go into business! I tell you, that in ten years you would make for yourself a competent fortune. And then with that you might retire from business, and be a student without being other than a sensible man."

"But for study I should then have lost all aptitude and taste. And also then I should have forgotten a thousand and ten thousand things with which I am now familiar, — facts, distinctions, characters of books, veins of feeling, principles of science, criticism, and philosophy, ways of expression, ancient languages —— "

"And so in order to retain all these things in your mind you are to forego, not only the certainty of a fortune, but even perhaps of a living. And for that who will thank you? Nobody! Who will think you a fool? Every body. And are you prepared for that?"

"I hope to be found so, if it is necessary."

"As a writer, you say yourself that you do not ever expect to be popular, or well paid."

"Uncle George, I would yield to your wish at once, if it were simply a question, whether I should get rich by such faculties as make an author popular, or by such qualifications as make a merchant successful."

"Now," said Mr. Coke, "now that there is an opportunity open to us, I think I can hear them calling to us, from their graves in Drayton church, — our forefathers, — not to fail of renewing for them that name which is fading fast, very fast. It is all now dwindled down to the few acres that are entailed, — the old estate. I did hope, in a few years, that I might myself have been able to buy back some portion of what was once our land, and particularly the fields called Sir Humphrey's Walk. I wish now that you would do what I cannot. Of mere preference as to your manner of life, I think you might be willing to forego something, merely for the satisfaction of raising again the old name in the old place. And you, Percy, surely ought to feel something of this, for you are both the youngest member of the family and also the head of it."

For a few seconds the young man was silent, and then he said, "The old name! It began with a new man; and if it is ever to be renewed again, it must be out of a new spirit. Once, for a name to be respectable, it was necessary it should be that of an estate, — the name of a man and his lands. But it is hardly so now; and soon it will be so no longer. Once, as perpetuity for a name, there was needed what only money can buy, — stone piled on stone. But now a name is not land lying wide and senseless under the shining sun and the midnight dark; nor is it a monument pointing with a cold finger up among the mists, and toward the clouds. But now a name is winged, electric; and it flashes from city to city, and to the ends of the world. And the honor of it is by the firesides at which it comes up. And the duration of it is according to the strength of the love that is in it."

"Perhaps, — perhaps so."

"Uncle, there is no one knows it better than you do, or feels it more."

"You think, Percy, I care little for the old ancestral spot. You are mistaken. True, I have never been at it for more than twenty years, and never hardly spoken of it; but it has been for grief, and shame, and mortification, not for indifference. And now, Percy, you wish to be a student for life. You hope to be a man of new, high thought. Suppose the best; and suppose you are. Then you will be a man of many enemies and no friends. You will open ways of thought. But at the ends of them other men will build monuments inscribed with their own names. And when you have died, you will be a good subject for a memoir."

"But fire from heaven —— "

"Draw fire from heaven, and with it light a lamp to guide your fellow-creatures, in their human darkness! Have not they got vicars, and rectors, and deans, and prebendaries, and bishops to direct them? Our Manchester merchants are the most likely men in all England for your purpose. Now among them it shall be understood that you are a man of a large, rare intellect by nature, and that by long years of faithful study you are a man still rarer. Do you think you could get fifty of them to attend to you, either by listening or reading? I tell you that you could not obtain five. Not five! For one man yields himself credulously to a domineering clergyman; and another mistakes in a preacher flexibility of tongue for quickness of thought, and depth of voice for depth of mind. And another indignant man would exclaim, 'Teach me! who are you? where is your money?' Fancy yourself now on the Exchange, among the merchants, your book in your hand. And what do you see? You see your prospects in life; and they are nothing."

"Hardly, sir, so ought one ——"

"You will publish your book, — the work of years, — thoughts which you have arrived at through agonies of belief and unbelief, through seasons of intense thought and exhausted strength, and all throughout by the help of rare genius.

And on a few hundred copies of your volume you will obtain perhaps sixpence for profit, reward, a living. And twenty times as much, perhaps, will be paid by every one of your readers to see a dancer on the stage, to hear an opera, to see the lady we call the Queen, to have a seat at a public dinner given to some general, or member of Parliament, or president of a company."

"But by somebody," said Percy, "it has got to be done, — the highest work of the world."

"But not therefore by you. Write biographies, write romances, write a book on cookery, compile an arithmetic. But do not do what people do not want. Genius entering into the temple of theology to meditate, — or ascending the heights of science and growing radiant in the face from talking with the Divine, — or sitting still to listen to the harmony in which blend together the music of its own thoughts and sweet influences from on high! For a man's happiness there is commonly no greater mistake than this, — nothing more woful."

"But, sir, where would be, what would be, the souls of men, but for the self-sacrifice of genius, — the courage of Milton in singing of Paradise Lost, careless even of the ten pounds which he did get for the poem."

"Sacrifice of yourself! Call your project by that name, and I shall be better satisfied. However, we will talk of this subject again. But I do wish you to understand distinctly what it is that you are doing. You are rejecting a fortune for the sake of study and poverty and fame and usefulness, — study and poverty during your life, and fame and usefulness after your death."

"And is that nothing? And would not it be much, even though in my lifetime only a thousand souls should have me for their benefactor?"

"Have you for their benefactor! But then they will not hold you so. Out into the world you will go, and before swine, and men, and dogs, you will throw down your pearls of holiness. And then almost it will be well for you if you are not noticed, for then at least you will not be abused nor persecuted. But the dogs and swine, and indeed most men, will walk among your pearls and never heed them. Now and then a pious man will find one, and he will call it, perhaps, the beauty of holiness. But on account of the casual way by which he becomes possessed of it, he will never think of you as the giver of it."

"But yet to have men indebted to one spiritually ——"

"Will not help you to live bodily. And certainly you have got to live, either in the poor-house or out of it. O, you will have men owe you every thing, and be indebted to you infinitely. And shall I tell you how much it amounts to, an infinite debt? Boundless love, and not one farthing. No, nor even the slightest service, nor the least compliance with you in any plan of your proposing. For, Percy, I know well what I am speaking about. For I have had the public indebted to me boundlessly."

There was a pause, and then the uncle began to talk of his own past life, — his actions, the motives to them, and how his soul had been acted on by untoward circumstances. And as in narrative the stream of his uncle's life flowed past him, Percy Coke saw in it his own likeness, sometimes distinctly, like an image deep down in the water, but oftenest like a momentary reflection lost in ripples and eddies. But anywhere, with attention, he could perceive his own image appear for an instant. And he sickened at the sight of its coming and going so painfully; yet he felt that he was growing wiser with it.

In conclusion, Mr. Coke said, "In choosing a way of life, a man ought to think, not only of the crown which he hopes to attain, but also of the thorns he must walk on. And if he cannot endure the thorns even to look at, then is it very certain that never will he pass through them to reach the crown, however pleasantly for a time his eyes may be dazzled with it. And, Percy, how it happens I do not know, but I have noticed it as a fact, that it is destructive of character, and indeed peculiarly pernicious, for a man to act on motives that prove to be too high for him, — to do a generous action and repent of it, — of his own choice and for the sake of religion to take up a cross to carry, and after a time to wish he could fairly drop it."

"My dear uncle George, you are so wise and good."

"All I wish, Percy," said Mr. Coke, "is to be sure that you understand what it is that you are doing in the decision you are now making. You can yet be a merchant. You are not yet too old to disjoin yourself from genius. But soon you will be. And it will possess you like a spirit. It will disable you from working for money or bread, or any other merely earthly motive. It will hold you to the service of high thought, — a service for which you will be laughed at, as moonstruck, by nearly every body, by rich men and poor men, merchants and peasants."

"That I can endure, I think. For already I have drawn upon myself all the pity and scorn possible, by being too honest to sign what I did not wholly believe, — the Thirty-nine Articles. Because by that scruple I was debarred of my degree, and of almost every successful entrance into life. Uncle, I know well that so often, in so many directions in this world, especially for its own profit, genius is powerless, even although it be free of the heavens, and of the regions whence flow down among men thoughts from eternal fountains."

"It is light and heat for the whole world, and yet it will hardly kindle a fire in a kitchen."

"A faculty, a possession, that is of use not at all in furnishing a house, but only in brightening it; and which avails a man very little in earning the means of life, but only perhaps in making common bread sometimes taste like 'angels' food.' Such is genius, I suppose."

"And now I think we understand one another," said Mr. Coke. "If only you do thoroughly understand its nature, then I would not dissuade you from your purpose in regard to a studious, literary life. For if a man might hope at last to speak but one enduring word of beauty or truth, then I think, if necessary, that he might well be like the Baptist, and dwell apart from the sweet, lively scenes of life, and feed on coarse and scanty fare, and have no loving eye to watch him, and in his spot on the desert meditate through all the years of his manhood, and till old age."

## XXVI.

NIGHT, night! O, there is something in us that is divine, and of which night is the high season! In the day we are surrounded with objects for the eye, but at night with the infinite, for the soul to feel and tremble at. And more so than in the bright day, out in the dark night we are souls to one another.

It was midnight, and at the window of his study the minister looked out into the night. And there came into his mind how, ages ago, a father of the Church had said, that it is the duty of spiritual doctors to rise up often by night, and think of the state of the Church, so as to discover how to correct things which have been defiled by sin. And then came upon his soul from the night the feeling of it, — mystery, awe, wonder, and fear, — that panic sensation with which every heart has some time throbbed. And he said to himself, "In the dark how close about us they feel, — the things of the spirit! By night it comes in upon the soul with such persuasion, — the Spirit of God; and they are to be heard speaking so tenderly, — the voices of departed souls. And in the dark, wise words of ages ago come up into our minds with a freshness like that of living voices." And then he remembered how for righteous men Clement called the night a veil of sweetness; and how Cardinal Bona had exclaimed, "O the peculiar prerogative of the night-time! O the holy hours of the dark, more splendid than any light!" Also he said over to himself the words of St. John of the Cross. And as he repeated them, he wondered whether he had himself then come through all the dark passages. "The perfect have to pass through the night of the senses, the night of the spirit, the night of the memory, and the night of the will; which four nights represent the four kinds of mortification which they must endure."

And as he looked in the direction of the town, he heard the church clock strike twelve, and the chimes play the tune of Old Hundred. And then he said over to himself, in the terse Latin of Columban, these sentiments of long ago. "O life! how many have been deceived by you! Nothing hardly in the passing, and only a shadow to remember! Day after day you fly, and day after day you are with us again. By coming, you pass away; and then having passed away, you are round upon us again. To look to, you seem so real; but to look back on, you are so merely fallacious! And therefore, O mortal life! fugitive as a bird, uncertain as a cloud, unsubstantial as a shadow, you are nothing, unless perhaps some semblance of what may prove to be a way."

And then he thought how serious a thing it was to be a minister, — in any way to have souls dependent on him for guidance past the broad road and along the narrow way to life eternal, — to be a theologian, and to have people rely upon his judgment on great, awful matters of the spirit, — to be a pastor, and to have men and women die in the faith of its being really Christian, the doctrine of his teaching. And he said, "This people dwell about me here. And to some extent, certainly, I am the eye which they see by, — the conscience they judge by, — the prayer by the earnestness of which their hearts express themselves, — and the wisdom on which they rely for being right. Do

I feel this as I ought, — as seriously as I ought? Do I study, and meditate, and pray as I ought, sanctifying myself for their sakes?"

Just then, swift, silent, and beautiful, there streamed down the sky a falling star. And the minister said, "Myself, O, not myself, I hope, I trust!"

That night he had a dream. Behind him there was a wood, inside which there was a sound of falling water. And before him the ground stretched away to a slope, along the bottom of which ran a brook. About him were flowers, some standing up like the tall lily, and some just to be seen at his feet creeping in the grass. Close beside him was a thick tree, that was like a hillock of gorgeous blossoms, from the ground to the top of it. And overhead was a sky of the softest, deepest blue. Amid all this beauty he stood entranced. But a voice cried, "Out of the heart are the issues of life." And then through his soul there flashed conviction, — a sense of pain, and shame, and sin.

About him there appeared objects which he felt had in them a something of his own nature. Embodied in emblematic forms, there were visible about him the thoughts and feelings of his own sinful heart, — things mournful and hateful, and ludicrous and strange, — a serpent on the ground, coiled up as though for a spring, — the fierce head of a dog barking and snapping from side to side, — a goose, his head aloft, hissing in the air, and his feet set in the mud, — thick mists hanging low on the ground, and blighting all things beautiful beneath, — a phantom man, with his face turned upwards for prayer, and his hands busy with a purse, — on the grass, moving about, a smiling human face, with a tail and a sting behind, — and in the air, floating about, shapeless objects that changed incessantly in loathsomeness from one vague form to another. From beneath, it was as though the firm ground had grown hollow. And from the wood behind him continually there blew out upon him cold blasts, with which his courage quailed in him and sank.

He strove to look abroad, but he could not; and up on high, to heaven, but he could not. For his eyes were drawn irresistibly to the hateful things about him. And it felt as though from within him his soul were longing and bending towards every loathsome object that he saw.

And he threw himself down, his forehead to the ground. And he cried, "God deliver me! because I cannot even see for my sins; and even my mind is defiled." And his whole soul flowed forth in prayer, fervent, effective. And he prayed, "Kill me, O God, if thou wilt. But leave me not to grow hateful with these hateful things about." So did he yield himself to God, and all his powers as instruments of righteousness to God. Then down from the sky a voice cried, "Sin shall no more have dominion over you."

He rose to his feet, and looked around. And he saw that it was become more beautiful than before, — the scene about him. And round him, on the ground, lay his late terrors lifeless. And it seemed as though they were melting and vanishing, — those phantom forms of sin; and as though from beneath them the flowers were springing up, sweeter to smell, and of richer colors. And while he was wondering at this, his dream ceased. And, half asleep and half awake, he said to himself, what George Herbert had said before, "So that the parson having studied all his lusts and affections within, and the whole army of temptations without, hath ever so many sermons ready penned as he hath victories."

## XXVII.

Martin May had been at Manchester for two or three days during the first week in October. He returned to the Dell, about the middle of the day, on Friday. With the exception of one old woman, he found all the inmates of the house were out. And from her all he learned about them was, that they were gone into the town. In the afternoon he thought he would himself go and call at the Parsonage.

It had been a fine autumnal day, and all the morning, along the roads and over the fields, there had been coming to Thorpe men and women, mostly young and wearing their Sunday clothes, and looking clean, and merry, and healthful. And in regard to the men it might have been noticed that in their hats they wore what might have been correctly understood to have been emblematic of their occupations, — a piece of whipcord, or some cow-hair, or a bit of sponge, or some flowers, or a little wool.

As soon as Martin May got on to the high-road, he saw that there was a great confluence of people towards one end of the town. He met a young man, looking like a farmer, and he asked him what it meant, — this great assemblage of strangers at such a quiet spot. The farmer answered him, "O, it is the hiring."

"The hiring! What is that?"

"Statutes is what we call it in Norfolk."

"Statutes! I do not understand?"

"Well, then, it is what is called a mop in Worcester, if you have ever been there."

"No; I have not. But why a mop?"

"Because there is a mop on a high pole, for the people to stand about, at the hiring. But go on a little way, and then you will see for yourself."

In the market-place there were ranged in rows more than fifteen hundred men and women; the men on one side of the cross, and the women on the other. Up and down, between these rows, walked the farmers and their wives, seeking for such men and women as they would need in their houses for the ensuing twelve months, — wagoners, shepherds, cowmen, housemaids, and dairy-maids. Among the women every now and then a girl would step out of the rows to talk with some farmer and his wife. Sometimes the girl would agree to their proposal at once, and receive a shilling for what was called earnest-money. And sometimes she would quickly decline an offer made her, influenced by some dissatisfaction, either at the amount of the wages, or at the expression of the master's eye, or at something shrewish in the voice of the mistress.

At first, with what he saw, Martin May was sad. But all round the outskirts of the assemblage there were such shouts and laughter, and ludicrous sights, that from them soon he caught the humor of the occasion. He went up to a very fat young woman, who held an umbrella in one hand, and a large bundle in the other. And he accosted her, as though he was a housekeeper desirous of her services, " Young woman, you are a ——"

" A housemaid, or housemaid and cook, sir. And if you please, sir, I can do a little plain sewing. And when there is a pig killed —— "

" And what can you do when there is a pig killed ? "

" Sir, I can help."

" And now I want to know about your cooking. What cakes can you make? Symballs, doughnuts, jumbles, cream-cakes, and buckwheat, molasses dough-cake, ginger cookies, can you make?"

"Please, sir, I can make oat-cakes, if they would do."

"Can you make griddle or hoe-cakes, or whaffles?"

"I think I could if I were to try. For please, sir, I can make oat-cakes well."

"Can you make a squash pie?"

"Squash! Please, sir, I do not know what it is?"

"Can you make a chowder? Do you know what is a tipsy parson?"

"Yes, sir; Parson Fuller, that used to live at the Glades."

"Ah, was he? And now should you know what to do with clams? Do you know how to cook hominy? Succotash, — do you know any thing about that? Succotash!"

"O, sir, I came from Tyldesley, and they have none of those things there. And I am sure, sir, I should not do for you."

"And I am sure I think you would, very soon. But, however, we will say no more about it. I will not hire you. But I will give you some earnest-money. Essentially our decision is philosophical, and as an arrangement it is more congruent with the nature of things than its opposite."

The girl took the shilling with a smile, and went back and stood by the side of her companion, and said to her, "Such a queer man he is! He asked me about all manner of outlandish things to cook. And what do you think? At last, he talked almost like that Frenchman, when we could not tell one word that he said, that day that you remember."

Martin May went on, down rows of girls and past booths, at which were sold sweetmeats, printed calicoes, combs, walking-sticks, whips, knives, ribbons, horse-medicines, halters, dream-books, mole-books, song-books, and books of receipts. He met several acquaintances, who laughed to see him there. Near the end of the last row of women there was a girl of a very pretty, innocent look. She seemed to be of a sweet, confiding disposition, and perhaps to be not without something of simplicity in her character. Towards this young woman Martin May felt himself benevolently disposed; for he pitied her, as she did not seem to have secured for herself an engagement. So he thought he would present her with some earnest-money.

"Young woman," said he, "you are a housemaid, I think."

"Yes, sir."

"And you are not hired yet?"

"No, sir," answered the girl, in a tone of some mortification.

"Where has been your last situation?"

"At Mrs. Lawson's. I lived there, sir, two years."

"So! And why are you leaving there?"

"Please, sir, we have all had to leave."

"Ah, all of you!"

"Yes, sir, five of us, three girls, and a man, and a boy."

"I hope there was nothing very seriously wrong among you."

"No, sir, not very. Though Mrs. Lawson cried. But she is not Mrs. Lawson now. And Mr. Smith said he could not and he would not live at the Pinfold, and that she must go and live with him at some grand place beyond London. And so she is Mrs. Smith now, and we do not live with her now."

"And what wages do you ask?"

"Eight pounds, sir, a year."

"I like your appearance very much. I think a woman like you would suit me well. There is earnest-money."

The girl extended her hand; but she was just going to ask a question, when Martin May gave her half a crown, and said, "Now you will have your things all ready against I want you. And I will meet you here in the village, and take you on, next Thursday."

The girl gazed at the handsome earnest-money, and asked timidly, "But where do you live, sir?"

"At Boston."

"I think I have heard of it. But is not it a long way off, in Lincolnshire?"

"O, no!" said Martin May, in a very earnest tone. "I will meet you here and take you down to Liverpool. And so then in a ship we will go to America."

At this the girl burst into tears and cried, "O, but I cannot go, please, sir. O dear, sir, I cannot go, I must not go. Not over the sea! O dear, dear, what shall I do? O, pray, sir, do take this money back. O dear, O dear!"

At this sound of distress up rushed a young man with a red neckerchief, and a red waistcoat. He drew the young girl aside, and planted himself before Martin May, and cried, "What are you doing to this young woman? Let me alone, Jenny. This is my business." And as he said this he clenched his fists and breathed hard. But a policeman laid his hand on his shoulder, and said, "Quietly, my man! What is all this noise for?"

Martin May turned to the young woman and said, "It would have been all a joke, only that you were so frightened. And that earnest-money was to pay for it. There! keep it. You deserve it, I am sure. And I only wish I had a home for you to come and live at. Good by."

Martin May walked on; and Jenny cried, "Thank you, sir; thank you, sir." And then she turned to the young man and reproved him. "O James, James, to think of your running up in that way, and laying hold of me so, before all the people! And then to speak in such a way as you did to such a good gentleman as he was! But you know, James, you always were so passionate! Always! But I do wish you would not be; for you see what a bad thing it is."

The policeman followed after Martin May and said, "Excuse me, sir. Squire Burleigh's footman asked me to look out for you, and to tell you that he had left a note for you at your lodgings. And he said he thought you would like to know of its being there. Curious people, sir, these countrymen, on a day like this, especially when they have had a little ale."

## XXVIII.

"So, Percy," said Mr. Coke, "so you are resolute to forego money and comfort, and you are intent on discomfort, and perhaps usefulness."

"Do not understand me as speaking more enthusiastically than I mean, and then, uncle George, I will try to let you know what I feel. Of myself I incline to this life of religious study, but also I think I am drawn to it. Sir, you are a religious man, and you believe that for individuals in private life there may be actions, and that for a nation in its history there may be sometimes a crisis, toward which a man may be led by guidance that is higher than human."

"Go on, Percy."

"I think religion wants a new birth, needs to be vitalized in the heart of some man peculiar either for genius, or for education, or for his spiritual experiences. However, for this effect I do not mean that any one man, or any ten, would be sufficient. At present, in the minds of men religion is weakened by science; and yet almost uniformly it is preached as though there existed no such thing as science. From the pulpit, on the subject of the Deity, sermons continue to be preached by men who are sublimely indifferent as to any thing that can be seen through the telescope, or any thing that can be inferred from the discoveries of geology or from the laws of chemistry."

"I suppose that is quite true of such preachers as you have oftenest heard."

"But though ignored by religious teachers, natural science makes itself felt in religious minds, and weakens for them their faith. And so now there is hardly a Scriptural doctrine which any man believes in now as he ought, in the ease of his soul, genially and undoubtingly. Science reads aloud to us from the great volumes of earth and sky, and points to objects about our feet, and to the stars overhead. And then ourselves afterwards, in reading the Bible, we believe as much as we can. Hardly now does any man believe in the God of our Lord Jesus Christ, except with his lips and from old habit; for all the thoughts of God that rise of themselves in his mind evince him to be really a believer in the God of Copernicus and Newton. The grace of God, — is not this fast becoming merely a figure of speech? We believe in the God of heaven and earth; but who is there that believes, and trembles, and walks, and rejoices, as though on his own shoulder were laid the hand of God, lightly, but unavoidably? Who is there that ever feels as though God were angry or pleased with him? And except in some few blessed moments, now and then, do not most persons feel as though their prayers went up into the empty skies, and not into an anxious, listening ear? Peace and joy in believing, — how rare they are! God! he is understood as being a God of the stars, — a God of electrical and chemical laws, — a God of uniformity, but not a God of souls; a God of men, all men, but not a God of men one by one, — not a God of a covenant, — not a God whom I can have for myself as effectively as though we were alone in the universe, — he and I."

"That is true, Percy, miserably true. And yet it had never occurred to me, at least not in the way you state it."

"Of course," said Percy, "I believe in science. But also I do believe that God reaches after me, as though with the arm of Christ, and that he speaks to me as though from the lips of Christ. Christ, — God in Christ, an everlasting revelation, — I do wholly and joyfully believe. From the stars of Orion, you may infer what the manner of the Divine power is among the stars of another constellation. But from what God is to the stars anywhere, you never can infer what he is to the souls that dwell in a planet, — souls that are not mere insensate matter, but creatures of freedom and thought and feeling. From the laws of nature, I can learn what God is to my body, but not what he is to my soul, — not all he is, and how he is. Not from the sky, nor out of the earth, nor from science, nor from human logic, but only from out of a soul, can I learn what God is to my soul, — only from what David felt and Isaiah showed, and perfectly only from Jesus the Mediator. Against all prejudices to the contrary, which originate with science, I do believe that like the manner of heart with heart is the way of God with each human soul. And in this faith I can pray prayers that are prayers, and I can meditate as though in solemn talk with God. And looking heavenwards I can open my soul and have it grow joyous, and holy through joy, and strong."

"I am listening with great interest," said Mr. Coke.

"I can foresee that soon against the world to come there will rise thick clouds of unbelief, in which men will have to walk as though in darkness. But myself I know of means for building a high tower of thought, by ascending which a man shall find himself shone upon by the Sun of Righteousness, and comforted by the healing in its wings. This tower, this church-tower, shall I not, ought I not to build it, if I can? Shall I decline this holy work merely for the sake of rebuilding an old house?"

"You shall do, Percy, altogether as you think right."

"I think, too, that I see how they are properly tenable together, some doctrines of religion which have been usually thought to be inconsistent, and of which one sect has taken one, and another sect another. Also I think I have some fresh perception of my own, as to the use of reason in religion, — how far and how far only human ways of thought are rightly applicable to the interpretation of Divine things. And, uncle George, I think also, as I have said before, that I have some ideas of my own on politics."

"No wonder it usually ends in stupidity, — a

college course which begins with having a boy sign the Thirty-nine Articles. But that natural result of your education I think you have escaped. And even if you had become a rector, and preached self-denial to a congregation of peasants, on an income of two thousand pounds a year, perhaps you would not have had your hearers be the worse for you, — be the more stupid. O the way some congregations suffer from some eloquent preachers! All intellect among them, for the time at least, dying a delightful death of inanity."

"As you know, uncle, I have never heard one of your speeches. And if I were still a Tory, I do not think I should wish to hear you, especially on your favorite topics of the Established Church, tithe, and church-rate."

"Rabid you think I am. But I know that I am not. Just now, Percy, you were speaking of the ill effects of science on religion."

"On the way in which, from scientific predispositions, it happens to us that our idea of God is that merely of a mechanical, and not an emotional Being, — how he is to us a great machine, wonderful, almighty, beneficent, but not our Father. Not a Being I can weep to, and for whom I can suffer, but only a machine so comprehensive and exact, as that to the perfection of it there goes every thing,— every grain of sand, and every star, and every thought of mine."

"Do not you think that often in philosophy it is something merely fortuitous which determines a man whether to follow Plato, or Locke, or Hartley."

"I think so. Once I was at a place called Weatheroak Hill, an eminence from which little brooks started towards the east and the west; one of them finding its way to the Irish Sea, and the other to the Trent and the German Ocean. And I think there is a point from which start various ways of philosophizing, and towards following either one of which a man may be inclined possibly by some casual circumstance, some mere matter of taste or feeling."

"So it always appeared to me. And therefore it seems to me such utter folly to accept the Scriptures as the records of a Divine revelation, and then to read them by the help of some philosophical system, libertarian or necessarian."

"O, but the fixed principles of philosophy, so demonstrably unchangeable! Such a sure foundation for a church! While really, at the bottom, there is nothing more fluid. It is as if some Christians of Abyssinia should build a church on a raft, — a church of width and height and beauty, and on it, high up in the air, the Cross. A church, a Christian church! But all the while beneath it flows the Nile, and sweeps it along down to Egypt, and into the midst of idolatrous things, or perhaps out into the Mediterranean Sea, an utter wreck."

"And O the many minds now," said Mr. Coke, "that are being swept away into scepticism, some from one cause, and some from another! Only to think that of the people of this country more than a half are living apart from every Christian institution! And of those who are really religious, how many there are who are distressed with doubts, miserably, perniciously! It is a serious matter to resolve on, — a life of such study as you contemplate. But as you say, it does seem almost as though you might be appointed to it."

"O my life! Five years I lived at Oxford, and was a gownsman there, and walked in all the pride and poetry and high pretence of her ways, only to have them at last feel some of them unreal, and some of them roads to gates which I could not honestly open. Three years I was a student at Bonn and Halle. And at those places every month I grew more and more learned, and less and less wise. And seven months I was ill at Cologne. And the time of that sickness was the time of my new birth. Then first I came to know of there being in me other faculties than the logical, critical, recollective, by the aid of which I had been studying. And there opened upon me views which I had been blind to before. And it seemed to me as though, like angels from heaven, great, bright thoughts came to me and talked with me. And O the trials I have passed through! At Oxford, when I drew back from signing again the Thirty-nine Articles, all over England every door of promotion fell to against me, with a loud crash. And my heart in me sunk at the sound. And at Bonn, O the agony of thought I had, and the way in which I wept for the earth, as having in it nothing more divine than electricity! O those dreary, weary months, in which I grew in knowledge and in sorrow! A wretched time of unbelief, during which I should never perhaps have prayed at all, but for a dear old habit, derived to me, without a day's interruption, from the time when I used to lisp simple awful words, with my head upon my mother's knee."

"You have had stranger experiences than I had thought, Percy."

"It is an age of such contending principles, and therefore necessarily of principles that are often only partially true. Often among religionists there are to be found men of vehement profession, and excited feeling; but so seldom a man calmly and thoroughly persuaded in his own mind. And whence this bewildered state of men religiously? Very largely it is because from science and history there is so much new information, of which it has not yet been settled whether it means any thing or nothing in religion; and if nothing, how and why it means nothing."

"And politically how strange things are! In Manchester there are the Tories, who hold by the right divine of the government to govern wrong, provided only it be done according to Tory maxims; and there are the Whigs, good, sensible men like myself, but who unfortunately have to follow some questionable aristocrats for leaders; and there are the Chartists, who want every thing changed, they do not know how, and who are furnishing themselves just now, every man, with an argument from the anvil,— a pike, a horrible instrument like a spear, with a hook on one side of it. And then, besides Tories, Whigs, and Chartists, we have those who believe that public matters will go right of themselves, some way, if there is no noise made. And also there are your old Oxford friends, who believe that every body and every thing and every movement must be wrong, that does not add to the stones or the gold of what they call their church. And so, there being such an opposition and contention and bewilderment in politics, I can well conceive how it may be in some other regions of thought."

"For those who start right, the way to the Temple of Religious Truth, and by the gate of Strong Conviction, may still be plain and unmistakable. But certainly it is not so for those who start from among such prejudices as I did. O my mental wanderings! I have walked in the shadows of the Catholic Church, and listened to music from some invisible source within it, and felt soothed and inclined to have my forehead crossed with holy water from the fount. I have sat in a school of philosophy, and learned to think that between right and wrong there is only the difference between convenience and inconvenience. And for a time I knew what it was to eschew some vices, not for being sinful, but only as being in bad taste. Following one guide and another, I have been so misled that I have stood on the edge of a precipice, and been inclined to throw myself off it, with words of Seneca and philosophy falsely so called. And I remember that once I wandered along side of the Rhine, and I sat down almost in the shadow of the old castle of the Drachenfels. At my feet, out of a piece of turf there came a worm, and then drew back into it again. And I said, 'It is an emblem of myself, — this worm in a clod. For what better is this earth, than a mere heap of dust for me to struggle in?' Yes, uncle, I do believe that I have walked through all the unbelief and the misbelief of this century. 'And when thou art converted, strengthen thy brethren.' These words were intended to reach beyond Simon Peter. They have reached my ear. And in a special manner they sound as though meant for me, now that I have come through so much scepticism, — now that I am in Christian daylight, — now that I can worship in the attitude of Jesus, and feel God looking at me, as though through the eyes of Christ, — now that I have come to the knowledge of the Mediator."

"Yes," said Mr. Coke. "Truth feels all the truer to a man who has once been without it. And out of a million persons, if we could know the one man who religiously thinks most correctly and feels most strongly, I suppose we should hold him absolved from many a common consideration of convenience and prudence, and bound to utter himself and let his soul speak for the good of the world. And I do not know but that to people bewildered you ought to say what you can for their guidance, — you having been brought into the light through such tortuosities and darkness. Doubt, unbelief, misbelief, the way to the truth, — I suppose you know them, now, as you could not have known them in any other way than by having been through them."

"O," said Percy, in a tone of some emotion, "O, there is an experience for the want of which no reading and no observation and no study can compensate, — the experience of a man who has lost the way of faith, and so wandered through regions on which the Sun of Righteousness never shines, and where the moon in the sky looks as though turned into blood, — the experience of one who has been astray from Christ, and who by seeking his own way has found himself bewildered among the foundations on which existence rests; and who has had to ask there, in tears, and agony, and with uplifted eyes and hands, 'Wherefore is light given to him that is in misery, and life unto the bitter in soul?'"

## XXIX.

INTO all the country about Thorpe Martin May continued to make excursions after antiquities of all kinds. And he felt, both in body and mind, the good of exercise, fresh air, and the quieting influence of nature. He loved to walk in narrow lanes, between hawthorn hedges, which sometimes met above his head and made a long, green roof. And he was fond of following footpaths through green meadows, and across brooks on stepping-stones, and now and then through some shady copse, only to see where he would be led to. He would sit down on a bank or a stile, and talk with children, or he would walk along side a ploughman at his work, or he would find himself thirsty at some cottage door, and in need of some woman's charity, or he would acknowledge the friendly nod of some farmer, and so slide into conversation with him.

He went to see the ruins of Elmsley Church, and saw tall arches standing on high in beauty, but with the ground about them all overgrown with briers and nettles. He went to the ruins of an old castle, and passed hours in walking round the dry moat, and climbing the embankments, and in gazing from the top of the tower over the adjacent country, marked all over it with hedges and streams, and every here and there with a clump of trees and a few houses standing together.

Of the churches which he went to see, one was of the twelfth century, and showed, carved round the porch, just discernible, the signs of the zodiac; and another was remarkable for its old door, covered all over with the heads of Scriptural personages. To one church he went a long distance, merely to see the poor's box in it. It stood on legs, and was shaped like the roof of a house, and had three keyholes in it. It was of the fifteenth century, and was clasped all round it and over it with iron bands. In sport, Martin May dropped a penny into it. But the sexton exclaimed, "Sir, you must not do that. Nobody ever does that now. It is clean throwing the money away. For there never has been a key to that box, at least not in my time, nor in my father's."

At another church, while he was walking about it, there came in the clerk and began tolling the great bell. It was the passing-bell. And it was the first time that Martin May had ever heard it. The clerk said, "It is for Jack Chew. And it is a good riddance of him. But as for the bell, he does not deserve it. But his wife, poor woman, says she should like to have him die respectably, and like every body else. And so she sent me word that he was dying, and must have the bell tolled."

He went to see a house of the age of Queen Elizabeth. And he noticed that, like many other large houses of that period, it was loyally built in the shape of the letter E. He sat against the rugged, gnarled trunk of an oak-tree, that was probably two thousand years old. It was a tree about which the Saxons of what was called the weapontake used to assemble with their arms, on there being given any alarm of an enemy. And he said, "What would this tree be on the Hudson or the Potomac? Worthless wood, and no more! Old, old! Things are old only against the human lives they have outlasted. The men of a thousand years ago, the Saxons who gathered together here with their swords and axes, where are they? And yet here stands this tree;

and out of its old roots still creeps up, under this rugged bark, life enough for a few leaves. Life in an oak-tree, — it is strong for a thousand years, and it will last even two thousand. But life in me, life in any man, — it quivers on the pulse awhile, a little while, and then it is still, it is vanished."

In the houses of the farmers and the gentry there were articles of interest for him, — an old chair of black-oak, with a head very elaborately carved in the back of it, — a set of Apostle-spoons, being common spoons, with the heads of the twelve Apostles on the tops of the handles, — a curfew which had been used for extinguishing the fire at eight o'clock in the evening, according to the law of William the Conqueror, — a peg-tankard, a wooden vessel with pegs of measurement inside for drinking by, — an hourglass, which had been found in a coffin, — a slip of parchment, a very ancient deed, on which was written in red ink the grant of a manor to some Norman, by William Rufus.

He journeyed to see the Devil's Spadefull, and found it was a round hill in the midst of a plain. Jacob's Ladder he went to, and found it was only a flight of steps down a steep bank. In a secluded spot, he sought out what was called the Lazar-house,—the hospital for lepers three or four hundred years ago, when leprosy was a European disease.

Other places to which he journeyed were a field on which there had been a battle during the civil wars,—the site of a Roman encampment,—a portion of an old Roman road,—a barrow, a mound of earth on the top of a hill, inclosing in it the remains perhaps of Danes, or possibly of ancient Britons.

One day he made a visit to a hospital, as it was called, being one of the many schools founded all over the country during the reign of Edward the Sixth. And he thought in that school the sixteenth century was even then not quite over. For the boys were dressed, each of them, with a blue cap, a long blue coat, blue small-clothes buckled at the knee, and with yellow stockings. And Martin May found, too, that the youths were fed and taught after a like ancient manner.

On one of his excursions he saw a high, strong pole, with an arm extended from the top of it. It was a gibbet, on which once there had been hung in irons the body of a poacher, who had killed a gamekeeper, in an affray one night in the woods. And as he looked at it, there occurred to him some of the strange words that are in the Runic chapter of the Edda. "If I see a man dead, and hanging aloft on a tree, I engrave Runic characters so wonderful that the man immediately descends and converses with me."

He went to a town at some distance for the purpose of seeing a man of nearly one hundred and twenty years of age, and who had seen the battle of Preston-Pans, on the last irruption of the Highlanders into England. Another man he went to see was Roger Dowbiggen, a farmer who owned and cultivated the same land of which his ancestors had been possessed before the Conquest. And he found that this man of ancient family, and even of some wealth, had never been twenty miles from his house, and had just sold, as old iron, a complete suit of armor, in which one of his ancestors had fought at Flodden Field, and which had been lying like lumber in the house, as the farmer said, for hundreds of years.

Also he came to perceive of his own knowledge, how inveterate is superstition, — what a life there is in any practice or thought which has once had hold of the public mind. He found there were still surviving traces of the ancient Phœnician worship of the sun, — distinct remains of the Roman celebration of the festival of Maia, — indications of the Saxon worship which had for its objects Thor and Woden, — and practices and beliefs which the fierce Norseman had taught, and yet also had trembled to tell of.

From some children he learned that on New Year's Day they buy blessing-cakes, with pence given them for the purpose, — that on Twelfth Day there are twelfth-cakes, very costly, and not often to be seen, except in the shop-windows of the confectioners, — that on Shrove Tuesday the church bell rings for an hour, as a signal for pancakes to be made in every house, — that on Good Friday, for breakfast, every body has crossbuns, — that on Christmas Day there is mince-pie, and that a person has as many happy months in the ensuing year as he eats different kinds of mince-pie.

Close by the Dell was a vivacious old woman, whom he often got to repeat old ballads to him, and old songs. But she was simply an old woman of Thorpe. And so in nothing of her repeating was there any thing to equal what the Norseman had professed. For he said, "I am possessed of songs, such as neither the spouse of a king nor any son of man can repeat. One of them is called the Helper. It will help thee at thy need, in sickness, grief, and all adversities."

But some help there was for him at this time in some very old lines, which had come into his mind he did not know how, nor how correctly.

"And there is peace without any strife,  
And there is all manner of liking for life,  
And there is bright summer ever to see,  
And there is never winter in that country,  
And there is great melody of angels' song,  
And there is praising them among.  
All these a man may joys of heaven call;  
And yet the most sovereign joy of all  
Is the sight on high of God's bright face,  
In whom there rests all manner of grace."

## XXX.

One day, when the minister was with him, Mr. Coke said, "I wish you to do me a favor, Mr. Lingard. I wish you to give me your candid judgment on the literary abilities of my nephew."

"I think of them very highly indeed."

"But what I want from you is your opinion, not as to his learning or industry, but as to his genius, if he has any. And whether he has or not, is what myself I cannot tell, because I am not so much a judge of genius as I am of cotton and cloths. Percy is an honest, noble man, and wishes to devote himself to a life of study, believing that so he can be of some service to mankind. Now what I wish you to do for him and me is to ascertain, not his principles of thought nor his learning, but his genius, if he has any."

"I will talk with him; but myself I am sure

I should have no confidence in any opinion which I might form about him in the manner you propose."

"But myself, sir, I shall have implicit confidence in your opinion. And so I hope you will give it me. But now you must talk with him in a way that will not let him speak from his memory, but only out of his heart or his inventive powers. I do not know whether I make myself understood. Do I?"

"Yes, sir."

"You know even better than I do, that with all men often, and with most men always and universally, conversation is merely a repetition of facts or sentiments which they have learned. And sometimes I have thought, in listening to a conceited and much admired preacher, that, if suddenly there were struck from his sermon all that was not his own, he would be left standing before his idolaters, a senseless idol, dumb and impudent."

"I have read," said the minister, "that if madder be given to an animal in its food, it may be found, in twelve hours, to have been so thoroughly taken into the system, as to have colored every bone in the body. Madder is traceable, though most other things which are eaten as food are not. And because proverbs are traceable, the conversation of my housekeeper illustrates your remark exactly."

"Yes, you understand me," said Mr. Coke. "And I would suggest that, in talking with Percy, you should lead the conversation to important subjects, but approach them from some unusual side, and not remain at any topic long enough for him to recollect himself, and so for him to begin talking out of his memory."

"Let him come to me to-morrow evening. Say to him that I invite him to come and sup with me. Tell him that I shall expect him by eight o'clock. And then by candle-light and the fireside, and during the genial hour or two that are after supper, we will have some talk together."

"I wish very much that he would succeed me in my business, and yet also I should be delighted to have him succeed me in the world as a reformer. Not that I would have him work in my way. No! I would have him do what I cannot do. This hand of mine is hardened and stiffened with wielding heavy weapons against the fortresses of wrong. But the intrenchments of oppression are now laid open. And in time they will, every one of them, be levelled with the ground. And now for the fresh work there needs a fresh hand, — a hand that can wisely guide a pen, — the hand of a man such as you might be if you would, — a man well acquainted with the lessons of the past and the tendencies of the present, — a man who can read, not books only, but the human soul, — a man who believes in God, and in the existence and power amongst men of certain laws of Providence, which must be kept by, — a man who knows how social institutions must be built, not without attention to those invisible but irresistible influences which flow through the minds of men, from some of the mysterious things of the spiritual world, such as evil and even the way it is thought of. Not that Percy is thinking of being a political writer. For I suppose his mental tendency is towards religious sentiment."

"Beyond all things, Mr. Coke, religion is political, is what organizes men. Keep men walking with God, earnest to follow him, and with very little thought about themselves, they will journey through life in perfect order. And because their faces are set in the right direction, they will find themselves perhaps quite unexpectedly falling into the most beautiful array. And all the more intently they look towards God, all the more wonderfully will they journey on together through life; multitudes of all ages and conditions moving along in a harmony that is divine. But let men grow irreligious, let them turn away from God, and then think, hope, try as they will, they cannot move but into anarchy. As to institutions, and tone, the character of society is very largely determined by the way or the no way in which God is thought of. Remotely, it may be, but yet quite certainly, the real statesman of the world is not an orator, however successful in persuasion, nor a lawyer, however eminent, nor a crowned monarch, but a theologian sitting among his books, alone with his heart, and with his pen in his hand."

"Right, Mr. Lingard. You are right. And I say it as my experience, my intense conviction, that the spirit of reform must be religious, in order to be rightly effective. No social change of any considerable character was ever made for the better, merely by the strength of logic, or the keenness of satire, or the decision of sudden enthusiasm, or even by the incitements of that common benevolence which thinks more of suffering than sin."

"Yes," said the minister, "for the spirit of public reform to be right, it must be reverential, as well as just. And it must not be mere weak love, but be thoughtful with the seriousness of history, and be not without some feeling of the mysteriousness of human nature. It is not of mere will, or legislative enactment, that abiding laws exist. And it is very certain that no nation ever did, or ever could, adopt by mere decree the institutions of its neighbors."

"No, never in all history, I believe. If you would introduce a new usage, or found a new institution, it must be adapted to the spirit of the times, and have upon it the sanction of the past. The past! what have I to do with the past?—so many a man asks. And he thinks he lives only from day to day, free at any time to be of a new temper, Chinese, Russian, or Dutch, and capable of fitting himself to any customs or ways of thought which he chooses. Whereas the greatest innovator, when he is himself and calm, speaks, thinks, feels, acts, very largely in the spirit of the past."

"Our social usages," said the minister, "run back through decayed towns and vanished cottages and fallen towers into the remote past. Our laws are derived to us from many generations, and are ours, not without an influence on them from the Norsemen of Norway, and the Saxons of Germany, and the lawyers and the Senate of ancient Rome. And in our statute-book there is not a little which might be traced through our English courts, and the bulls of the Pope, and the tribe of Levi, to Moses in the desert, with the twelve tribes encamped about him."

"Yes," said Mr. Coke, "since I have been ill I have thought much on the political tendencies which myself I have done not a little to advance. I have reflected on the manner and consequences of some of our successes, as reformers. I have read the history of the Roman empire, and I have studied carefully the history of France. And more and more I think it essential in a statesman, that there should be a humble recognition of Providence in national history, and a strong feeling of man's spiritual relations towards God and another world. Equality and brotherhood! have the French people been crying these seventy years. They have enacted brotherhood by the will of the republic, and they have engraved it on every public building. But all that is meant is a brotherhood in dust simply, — the equality of creatures that are merely mortal; and so it does not last, and cannot."

"No, no! Mr. Coke. The ways of the world are not to be straightened simply as between man and man, but only when looked at as lying in the direction of God."

"That is the truth. And it is the great moral of all history."

The minister continued: "An undevout philanthropist may have a successful career among men, as a popular orator. And a parliament may debate by what legislative contrivances peace may be best maintained among the different classes of society. But for harmonizing discordant men, there is what is more effective than the oratory of mere benevolence, or the cunning of shrewd legislators. And it is this,—simply this,—from a man of intellect or genius, one devout thought uttered aloud."

## XXXI.

"Well, Mr. Percy," said the minister, as he stirred the fire, "it is a frosty evening, and so the fire burns blue, and is very comfortable to feel and look at."

"My uncle to-day has been expressing to me his great admiration of you, and says he owes you much gratitude."

"He is a gentleman in whom I have a great interest. I am glad to see you looking so well, Mr. Percy. But I had hoped you would have come a little sooner."

"On my way here I called at Mrs. Heywood's, and while I was in conversation time went faster than I was aware of."

"I am very glad to see you. For I am not well; and yet I am not ill. All day I have been unable to fix my mind on any subject of thought. And now this evening I am just in that state when a companion is most agreeable."

"I cannot," said Percy, "I cannot but admire this library of yours. As a room it is not too large nor too small. And from the windows you have such a fine view of the country in the day-time!"

The minister leaned back in his chair and said, "And at night, when there is stillness all about me, my library is the wonderful gateway by which I am admitted into the Past. Books, books! To handle, they are paper and paste; but to read, they are magic, thought, sight. O, by the help of these books what wonderful things I can do, especially at night! I can go back into past ages. I can walk on the banks of the Tiber, while Cæsar floats down it in his barge. I can go to the Colosseum, and find it roofed in and filled with tens of thousands of Romans; and I can enter the hall of a Tusculan villa, and listen to Cicero talking with his friends. At Athens I can sit in the amphitheatre, while some comedy of Aristophanes is acted; or I can go into the garden of the Academy, and hear great men talk their wisest. In Egypt I can see ruinous cities standing in their early strength, and thronged with inhabitants, busy, lively, and excessively idolatrous; and I can see the priests, robed in linen, walk between rows of obelisks and sphinxes, and past inscriptions, such as only they themselves can read; and I can see them in the temple make a religion of feeding the sacred animals, an ox, a dog, a cat, a crocodile, an ichneumon. Or I can walk the streets of Nineveh along with the prophet Jonah, and see the vastness and the temples which he saw, and also the winged lions, and the wheels within wheels, of which Ezekiel speaks. Or I can become a guest in Scandinavian homes, and hear the sea-kings tell of their fights, or some woman repeat a Saga of the old times, or some poet recite his fresh verses."

"So often," said Percy, "they are the common things of life, which are the most wonderful. And books are the simple means by which God lends us a glance that has in it something of the wonder of his own omnipresence."

"The Egyptians deified some animals, or at least held them as symbols, which they might use in the worship of the Divine. Lately, I have been thinking on the subject of animal life. Often now I think we men are reluctant to allow to the brutes the properties which really belong to them. We are slow to admit in them the existence of any semblance of reason; as though we were afraid it might vanish, — the distinction between us and them; and so we might possibly have to walk among them consciously discrowned, and lords of them by might only, and not by right. Justus Lipsius, in his eulogy, says that he has made out the elephant to be human, and endowed with discourse, reason, passions, and virtues. And though evidently what he says is exaggeration, yet it is unpleasant to read."

"Looked at from the doctrine of materialism, and indeed from some positions in life, men and brutes, as compared together, do not always suggest the pleasantest thoughts about our human nature. But there is an error in the mode in which often our human life is estimated. For in the common way of regarding him, man is only an imperfect brute. Look at a mob of men and women; or listen to twenty men, while they are talking and drinking and smoking at an inn; and then say whether these human creatures are so very much better than a herd of deer, grazing together so gently, and going in and out among the trees so beautifully, and all the while breathing the fresh air so sweetly. Simply to look at, thousands and millions of men, and indeed most persons, had better have been almost any animals than what they are. O, to sit in the woods, on a summer's day, and to hear the wood-pigeons coo! What peace there feels to be in the tree-tops! Doves have a way of life to live by. And from that is their peacefulness. And if we men were bound to a way of life, we should be as happy as the doves are. But we are not so bound; we are free. And our sins, — they are the aberrations of a nature left free in life, — free with a freedom which is awful to think of, because it is accountable in some way, somewhere. And our restlessness, our craving, our discontent, — this longing, which religion does not extinguish, but only consecrates, — what is it? It is the soul which is in us, unable to quite domesticate itself in this earth, even in the happiest circumstances."

"Yes, Mr. Percy, it is as you say. And what is most distinctive in man is not so much in any one faculty of his nature, as in the freedom of it. But yet you would not allow that they are right, who would impugn the preëminence of man above the beasts, even with regard only to the outward manifestation of his faculties."

"No, certainly I should not. O, sometimes it is asked, Is man's sagacity so much greater than an elephant's? or his constructive skill so much superior to a bee's? And then is not a dog teachable? And sometimes plainly does not he reason?

And in a rookery, is not there social order, and even a sense of justice? Be it so; and let all human powers be found, one in one beast, and another in another. Yet a man is not the less a man for that, any more than the earth is the less divinely shaped, because the nest of a piefinch is as round as a circle mathematically made. And after all that can be said, if there is reason in animals as well as in men, there is so with a difference. It is very certain, that, in some sense, the diamond and coal are the same thing; yet still, some way or other, the diamond is diamond, and coal is not it, and cannot be."

"Usually we think of animals almost only for what they are to ourselves. But this is unsatisfactory. For though some animals are serviceable to man, yet most of them are not. And so I often feel very strangely about them. They are fellow-mortals with us. And why are they what they are? If they live only to grow old and die, why are they alive at all? Some dogs and some horses, I have fancied, have known of their humble state, and felt the lowliness of it. And hardly any animal cries are altogether joyful, but a little sad. And there is something of a pensive appearance in the movements of most beasts and birds."

" To me," answered Percy, " it is as though the brutes could not have been any thing better than they are, or they would have been created so. For there is not a bird, which myself I could not have let be an angel, nor a dog, but I would have be human. A Newfoundland dog is a strange creature to be living in a planet so wisely made as our earth is. For why should not it have been humanly shaped, — why, and again why? It was not to be so: and therefore it could not be. And what occasioned that creature to be only a dog, has made me be what I am. Perhaps if that dog could have been rational, myself I might have been more than human. And could any other creature anywhere have been less limited than it is, then perhaps my own nature might have been larger. If the instinct of the dog could have been reason, then perhaps the lion and the lamb might have lain down together, and man might have talked with angels. Ah, yes, I am what I am, perhaps because the horse and the dog are what they are. My own nature is so very poor to what it might have been. And this I am reminded of, whenever I look thoughtfully at the cat on the hearth, at oxen in the fields, or at birds searching the hedges for food, or at May-flies fluttering about for an hour or two at sunset, and then dying. There is nothing but intimates that this is a world in which the Creator withholds himself, — restrains his almightiness. And, — as I often say to myself, — O the mystery, the wonder of it! And O the awfulness of it!"

"I can tell why a man ought to suffer; but I do not know why a brute should. An animal walking about in pain distresses me, and sometimes appalls me. But I say to myself, that there are more good and wise things intended in the universe than I know of; and that, no doubt, the cries of poor animals enter into the ears of the Lord of Sabaoth, as well as the cries of oppressed laborers."

"My theology," said Percy, "was once of such a nature, as quite to quail at animal suffering. And I used to try not to think of it. But now there is nothing in nature I should not be willing to know of. Though I am still sensible of the mystery which there is in creation. Lambs frisking in the grass are a pretty sight, and they make one say, "O, how good all things are!" But it is not so pleasant to think of a sheep worried in the night by a dog. I shall never forget how I felt when a friend told me of his having seen in the Atlantic an iceberg with a bear upon it. The poor bear was famishing, and was drifting away to the south and a wretched death. When I was told of the poor animal's cries, it was as though I had heard for the first time of the whole creation's groaning and travailing in pain together. In this earth it is not we ourselves only, we men, that suffer, but also all other creatures. It is a suffering world in which we dwell. But certainly it is for some divine purpose that we are in it. All creation suffering about us! Does it sadden us to think of? It does; and no doubt it was meant to do so; but also to affect us with a sorrow not hopeless or passionate, but solemn and sublime almost."

"Mr. Percy, it is by such subjects as this on which we have now been talking that I feel so gratefully what it is to be a Christian. This subject of animal suffering, — it is darkness into which revelation does not reach. And in it I walk utterly helpless. And so when I return to Christ I believe in him all the more willingly and implicitly for knowing of that moral night in which all those things lie, towards which he does not look. However, I think we miss of some right feeling about the brute creation, by regarding animals simply as objects useful or useless to ourselves. Use, — what use are they of? In us, what arrogance it is to be asking this about any living thing whatever. Gnats in the sunshine, — of what use are they? Now is any man the maker of them, that we should criticize them after the same manner that we do ploughs or mills? O, but if other creatures are made without a purpose, then perhaps we ourselves are. But is it right for us to feel bewildered in our little minds, because every thing about us does not tell us of what use it is. Usefulness is no standard by which for us to be testing creatures. We men, we ourselves, — of what use are we in the universe of God? None, none at all; any more than the sparrow in the garden, or the worm in the ground, or the grub coiled up in a leaf on the bush. But let them make me feel this way, this humble way; and then to me at least they are useful, — every living thing, the cow in the pasture, the bird in the air, and the worm underneath the sod."

"They are creatures of God, like ourselves," said Percy, "and so are fellow-creatures of ours. It is a lowly fellowship which we have with them, very. But it is good for us to feel it. And I think as you do, that about birds and animals there are some right ways of thinking and feeling of which we are not possessed. Animalcules, so small as for there to be millions of them in a drop of water, — minnows, that live and die in the same little nook of a stream, — moths, that flutter about in a garden for a few hours of a summer night, — insects, at home in the cup of a flower, — wild bees, that work so loyally, and winter together so snugly in banks and hollow trees, — ants, in their underground chambers, — living things, in the depths of the sea, — about these, and all other creatures of God, there is a way of feeling which would be good for us, religiously good, if only we knew what it was. And perhaps some time we shall come to the knowledge of it, when we feel more humbly than we do, and perhaps are more tender than we are yet towards the animal creation."

"St. Ambrose," said the minister, "would teach us that in animals we ought to see painted images of most of the virtues, set forth by God to remind us of our duties. And Philip Melancthon says, that in what is right and what is base, in what is useful and what is not, and in what is proper, the life of the ant instructs us better than Chrysippus or Crantor, the philosophers. Go to the ant, thou sluggard, says one of the Proverbs. And I think for wisdom and for pleasure we might look to the creatures about us oftener than we do. A great, very great pleasure some of them are, sometimes, for me to look at."

"I remember, sir, the singular, the very peculiar delight, which I once had so. One May evening I sat in a garden, seeing how beautiful all things were, and breathing the warm, sweet air. The beetle droned in the twilight; and some of the latest birds were still singing about, — the hedge-sparrow and the thrush. And I felt how sweet a thing it is, sometimes, only to live and breathe and listen. Then a bat flittered by me, close by me. And when I looked up, I saw three bats flying about a blossoming plum-tree. And they flittered among the white branches so prettily, clinging to them every now and then. And while I was looking up at them, I clasped my hands and said, 'O blessed little creatures! And God loves you too, and is the life of you.' And myself, just then, I loved them; not as I love knowledge, or beauty, or men, but another way, a new, strange way. And I think it may have been something of that way by which God is happy in all things."

"Yes," the minister said, "and in that sympathetic mood of yours we men should be different objects than what we are to one another. Members one of another, — down through those words from Paul's heart, what an everlasting stream of sympathy there flows! What a fountain of meaning there is in them! Do not you think so? Have you ever happened to reflect on them? There are no such words anywhere out of the Bible. In the Church, and indeed almost in any body of men, if one member suffer, all the members suffer with it."

"Or if they do not, they ought to, through sympathy. It is the way of nature, it is an ordinance of God for the good of our souls. All sufferers suffer for me; at least all do that I know of. In every weak man it is hinted to me, 'This is what thou wouldst thyself be, but for the greater strength of God which is in thee.' In the darkness of a blind man, I know to what a sad misfortune I have myself been created liable. In the outcries of an epileptic, I can hear it said to me, 'This dreadful thing dost thou escape only by the grace of God.' And when slowly, slowly a man is dying, and I see it, then I feel in it a solemn intimation, 'This way, this very way, thyself thou art going, only perhaps a little more slowly.' And thus every dying man and every sufferer is a sight to solemnize me; and he makes me feel how serious is that inner world from which my soul is fed."

"That inner world! Our outer world would be simple enough, were it not for the mystery of that inner world. This morning I read in Pindar a few words which sounded so strange, so exactly heathenish. He says that we ought to seek from the gods things suitable to mortal minds, as we know what our nature is for the present. And then he exclaims, 'O my soul, do not aspire after an immortal life; but apply to the labors for which you are qualified.' How strangely it sounds; does not it? And as though really, and in itself, he did know what life is, any more than what death is, or immortality!"

"Men often feel like Pindar still," said Percy, "and indeed we all do a little, at times. We think that death looses us from our old certainties. But those old certainties are merely our ignorance. I know all about my house and garden; and I know all the lanes in the neighborhood, and how they lead; and I know under what hedge the first cowslip blossoms; and in what bank to look for the earliest violets. And I know the brook, and every winding of it, and the still places in it, where the water-flies are. All about I can tell how the fields lie toward one another; and I can tell how the parish lies in regard to all the adjacent parishes. And from all this I fancy that I know where I live, — whereabouts. But really what is this knowledge? It is almost nothing. For what I live on is a spot amid infinite space. And in infinity I cannot tell whereabouts I am. I do not know whether I am near where the first world was made, or far from it. I do not know whether I am comparatively near the outside, or in the very midst of the universe. My own neighborhood, I feel at home in it, so thoroughly; and I know every side of it, — north, south, east, and west. And I never think how this familiar neighborhood belongs to infinity, and so has really no north, or south, or east, or west. And out of a million directions, I do not know which would be the shortest by which to get outside of the stars that shine around and above and beneath us. Ah, when I think that I know whereabouts I am in the universe, really it is only as the insect feels itself at home in the cup of a flower, knowing nothing of the plant itself, nor of the ground it grows in."

"Insects in a flower, with the stalk rotting beneath, or with a worm at the root! — that is what we are. We build, and reap, and hoard;

we covet more and more land to walk on, and call our own; but never think that somewhere it must break in, and we fall through and find our grave. I wonder how it would be, if never we had any expectation of death, if we came up against death blindly as the beasts do. I think then we should be different creatures from what we are now, Mr. Percy."

"Yes, sir, it is the end of life which makes life be so serious. To-day I can lose, and to-morrow I can trifle away, but not my life, not all life, not the whole of it. O, at the end of existence, I could wish to have realized something spiritual, — some abiding thing, — something in its results which will last longer than a day's pleasure, or a year's manual work. Pots and pans, and most of them worn out, — if a tinman can point only to these, as the sum of his life, his thought and care and toil, then it is a poor thing. And it is a poor thing if a farmer has to say at the last, 'These fields I have ploughed a hundred times over; and of the life I have lived, all the effect, the whole surviving effect to me, is in the good state of the soil.' And a very sad thing it is, if an old man holds a purse of gold, and has to think to himself, 'In this purse is the essence of my life. These yellow coins are all by which in any way I am the better for the struggles and anxieties of my lifetime. I have worked and I have suffered much. And now from it all I am this much the better, this purse of money.' A purse of which death is just going to make him let go!"

"Yes!" said the minister. "And then to think that it is out of our thoughts and actions that there are twisting what will be the leading-strings of posterity! Mystery. Only a little way, and then every thing runs into it. Responsibility, — there is hardly any thing but makes us feel it. The past, — it is for ever and ever coming over and over again. And the more thoughtfully we live, the more conscious do we become of powers which our souls live by, mysterious, awful. How, by what means is it, that we think or remember? A dream, — how wonderful it is for its accurate presentation of things, and almost always for its vividness, which is commonly more intense even than that of our waking sensations."

"I had quite forgotten," said Percy, "what a great loss I had when my mother died. But I know now what it must have been. For the other night I dreamed I saw my mother. She was ill, and looked so. And I thought to myself,

'Certainly, this is my mother; still her look is not what I thought it had been; and yet it is of the same expression as my aunt's. I thought you had been more beautiful; and yet you are, — O, yes, you are very beautiful.' Then my mother smiled, as though she knew what I was thinking. And she said, 'You know, Percy, I have been ill a long while.' And I said, 'O my poor mother, you are very ill.' And I bent my head towards her neck. But O the feeling with which I did so! I awoke with it. All through the next day I felt it, — so strange, so sweet. And it did not quite fade from me for nearly a week."

"A beautiful, happy dream! I wish I could have such a vision of my mother. She died when I was only ten years of age; and yet still at times I seem to feel lingering on my nerves the dear rapture of her embrace. Myself I seldom have a dream. And perhaps on that account such a vision is to me the more curious. However, I do not wonder at the way in which the ancients were impressed by dreams. For they seem to me gateways, — perhaps very fantastic sometimes, — but yet openings, by which there reach us glimpses of a mode of life other than this of the five senses."

"Why, how late it is!" said Percy, as he looked at his watch. "And how discursive our conversation has been, though not unpleasant, and I hope not unprofitable. I have felt myself borne along I hardly know how, out of one field of thought into another, and up heights of speculation, and every now and then into some shady place, and the presence of some ancient father, grave, and earnest, and decisive."

"It has been said by some one, perhaps in reference to something like what you have just expressed, that the soul becomes philosophical of her own accord, and she wonders at her own thoughtfulness, and the richness of her reveries afford her delight, and then she ascends from herself to her Creator, from earth to heaven. This evening we have been talking on a very interesting subject. And, Mr. Percy, I like your remark on the freedom of the human will. And myself, I would say this, — that to me it is a great token of my heavenly relationship to be sometimes — as the beasts never are — lost in life, bewildered in thought, and in want of guidance from on high."

## XXXII.

At the Parsonage the housekeeper opened the study door. The candles were lighted. And for a little while she waited as though for some moment when the minister might relax his attention to a large volume on the table, over which he was bending. At last she said, "Please, sir, in the pump the bucket does not draw well. Penny wise and pound foolish, they say; and so it had better be attended to at once. I am sure I do not know what we should do without water. And so I think it is a great blessing. Do not you think it is, sir?"

"Yes, a great blessing."

"A very great blessing, sir."

The minister looked up from his book, and said, "Yes, very, very great. For without it there could be neither cider nor rainbows."

Mrs. Satterthwaite looked a little mystified,

and then said, " Please, sir, I think that Mr. Percy Coke is making love to Alice Heywood."

" Indeed," said the minister quickly. " But it can hardly be so, I think."

" But, sir, it is so, I am almost sure."

" O, you must be mistaken, surely. For, Mrs. Satterthwaite, myself I have never seen any signs whatever of what you mention."

" That may be, sir. But years know more than books. And besides, I have been young myself. And though I have never had much education, yet I can tell, for being right in some things, that experience without learning is better than learning without experience."

" Alice Heywood! Let me think. Can it be? And yet it must. She is nineteen, twenty —— "

" Yes, it is quite true that time and tide stay for no man."

" And then Mr. Percy is an honorable, good man."

" Yes, sir, so he is. It being, as they say, that a man like a watch is to be valued for his goings."

" O, but Mrs. Satterthwaite, you must be mistaken, certainly. Because from what he is thinking of, — Mr. Percy Coke, — why should he — why should he be doing as you say?"

"As to what he is thinking of, I cannot tell. But as the old proverb is, a man would not be alone even in paradise."

"And now," said the minister, "tell me what it is you have heard."

"Nothing. That is, I have not heard any thing; because I have not spoken with any body about it."

"Well now, I was sure it was all fancy."

"O," said Mrs. Satterthwaite impatiently, "words are but wind; but seeing is believing. And though, to be sure, it was not much that I saw, yet you may know by a penny how a shilling spends. This afternoon I went to Mrs. Heywood's ——"

"But this afternoon Mr. Percy was to have ridden over to Drayton."

"But beauty draws more than oxen, they say. And this afternoon he was at Mrs. Heywood's. He must have been, for I saw him going away from there. I went in at the parlor door to speak to Miss Alice; and though she was alone, she did not notice me. But though she was sitting by the fire, she was looking towards the window. And through the window, down the alley, I saw Mr. Percy Coke going out at the garden gate. Love is the loadstone of love. And from the way Miss Alice looked, happy, and yet very serious, I can tell what she was thinking of. And I could hardly help standing still to look at her; for she was such a beautiful sight."

"Was that all, Mrs. Satterthwaite? But surely in a mere look you may have been so very easily mistaken."

"Please, sir, you can read Hebrew by the look of it; and I cannot. But there are some things which I am able to read by the look, because I have learned how. And then, besides, lookers on see more than players. And so I am sure I am right. Well, when Miss Alice saw me, she started and blushed. And then at once she began to talk to me, as though she had not blushed or started at all. But though the cat winked, she was not blind. And I said to myself, that with foxes one must play the fox. And so I did not let her know that I had noticed her blush."

"And," said the minister, "I hope you will not let any one else know."

"Of course not, sir. But I thought it was right to tell you what I had noticed. Miss Alice is a very kind, sweet, good, religious young lady; and Mr. Percy is an excellent gentleman. And so for once I do hope the course of true love may run smooth. Though I suppose it never does. For a man's best fortune or his worst is a wife; though, as they say again, patience is a plaster for all sores. And all is well that ends well. And yet, too, a good wife is the workmanship of a good husband."

## XXXIII.

One afternoon in November Martin May knocked at the door of the study in the Parsonage, and went in.

"I am glad to see you," said the minister, "I have seen nothing of you for a week. I wonder where you have been."

"I have been to see the ruins of Kirkstall Abbey. I stayed there two days. The last day I remained chiefly for the sake of returning to Manchester with a person I met there, and whom I had seen in Manchester several times. He was on a visit at Kirkstall. And I stayed for him a day, simply because he urged me. For indeed, besides his urgency, he had no other persuasive quality. I can say truly, that his conversation was not very various nor very exciting. He manifested an intense interest in the cotton market, and a thorough belief in his having obtained what he called vital religion. He described his religion so often as being vital, that at last I asked him to call it real or spiritual. But he would not, for he said that those epithets were but dead words, and not at all what he meant. His name was Bamforth. But it is not likely that you should know any thing of him. Why I have called just now is to tell you that I have received your note inviting me to tea this evening. But I will not stay now, for if I did I should interrupt you. And I am going to take a walk."

"Are you? Then walk with me. I am going in the direction of the Holy Well. I am going to a funeral. And, indeed, you may as well go with me. For the friends there will take your attendance as a compliment; and the more so, as you are an American."

"Whose funeral is it?"

"Joseph Halliwell's. He was a man of threescore years and ten, and ten more. He was eighty years of age."

"A very old man."

"Hardly so. If age means merely years, then he was old. But if it means feebleness, then he was not old. For one month ago he was a happy, ruddy, hard-working man."

At the cottage of the deceased man there was a great number of persons inside; and outside there was quite a crowd of people sitting on benches. Besides his neighbors and acquaintance, who were waiting to attend the funeral of the old man, there were present quite a large number of his children and grandchildren, and even his great-grandchildren.

Martin May was asked if he would look at the old man in his coffin. There had been just taken off his breast a pewter plate full of salt. And Martin May wondered at what the meaning of it might be.

A young woman, who was a grandchild of the old man, brought her little boy into the room, and held him up to touch the old man's head. And the child then said in a whisper, "Mother, he does not speak. And he does not know that I am Willie. And he keeps his eyes shut."

An old man standing by said, "Poor thing! he does not know what death is." And upon this, in a corner of the room where she sat, the aged widow began to weep afresh. But the minister laid his hand upon the speaker's arm, and said, in a deep, gentle tone, "And we, too, have to become as this little child, and not to know what death is; because for Christians there is no such thing, as is now made manifest by the appearing of our Saviour Jesus Christ, who hath abolished death, and hath brought life and immortality to light through the Gospel."

There were carried round among all the persons present trays full of evergreens, such as box and rosemary. And of these each person took a sprig, and held it in his hand. When the funeral procession was formed, the minister and Martin May walked in front of the coffin; and behind it there followed, two by two, nearly three hundred persons.

It was one of those still, silent days, of which there are a few in November, when cobwebs in the hedges hang motionless, and when every chirp of a bird is heard. The funeral procession moved on slowly and silently. But on approaching tho chapel, a few of the mourners began to sing. And soon, down the whole length of the procession, every body was joining in a funeral hymn.

The coffin was taken into the chapel, and laid on a table before the pulpit. There was a religious service. And then the coffin was taken out into the yard. But before it was lowered into the grave, a person approached and laid on the head of it a circlet of flowers.

After the body was laid in the ground, and the last prayer was concluded, every person came up to the grave and dropped into it his bit of evergreen, and so retired. While this was being done in silence, Martin May had his attention drawn from one gravestone to another. And there came into his mind some lines which he had read once: —

"What thou art reading o'er my bones,
I 've often read on other stones.
And others soon shall read of thee,
What thou art reading now of me."

In the evening, at tea, the minister said, "Here, take one of these cakes, and tell me what it is."

"It is pretty good; and it is very small."

"It was larger when your English ancestors knew it."

"How do you mean?"

"To-day! Tell me what is to-day. But as you have been away during the past week, perhaps you have not heard any mention of it."

"But to-day, sir! What is to day?"

"It is Farthing-loaf Day. And you wonder what that means. I will tell you. A long while ago, when a farthing was perhaps ten times its present value, there was bequeathed by some person a fund, from the annual interest of which there was to be given to everybody born in Church Street a farthing loaf. When Elizabeth was queen, or even when Charles the First was king, a farthing loaf was something to handle; and now it is hardly a mouthful; it is only one of these little cakes.

"But still it is a loaf, and still it is given, after all these ages. Astonishing! Farthing-loaf Day!"

"And on this day, too, for all the householders in Church Street, from a fund, which is only of the last century, there is a supper of bread and cheese and ale. The householders take it in turns, to receive the yearly interest of the fund and furnish the supper. And at supper, each man is directed to drink as a toast, 'Peace and good neighborhood.' This year, the entertainment is at the house of my friend, Marmaduke Wyvil. And I have thought you might like to see it."

"And so I should, very much."

"And what else is to-day, do you know?"

"No, sir; I do not. But I shall certainly remember it as Farthing-loaf Day."

"An antiquarian like you not know the festival-day of him who would have been your patron saint, if you had been a Catholic!"

"Is this St. Martin's day?"

"Yes. And it has really been a day in what used to be called St. Martin's Little Summer. A little summer! And they do really feel so, — the two or three fine days which we usually have about the eleventh of this month."

"At dinner to-day we had a goose, which my host, the farmer, called a Martlemas goose. I wished to know what it meant. But all I could learn was, that it was a Martlemas or a Martinmas goose."

"In the old Norway clogs, as they were called, or wooden almanacs, the day of St. Martin is marked with a goose. It is said to have been in commemoration of his having been discovered by a goose, when he had hid himself in some secret place, because of his being unwilling to be made a bishop."

"And when was that?"

"Fifteen hundred years ago, at Tours. Martlemas is one of the days which farmers date by, as I dare say you know. It used to be a day of many pleasant usages. And still it is a season of some little rejoicing. There is an old ballad on Martlemas."

"O, do you know it? If you do, I wish, sir, you would repeat it. Will you?"

Then the minister recited the following lines: —

"When the daily sports be done,
Round the market-cross they run,
Prentice lads and gallant blades,
Dancing with their gamesome maids;
Till the beadle, stout and sour,
Shakes his bell and calls the hour.
Then farewell lad, and farewell lass,
To the merry night of Martlemas."

"And now," said Martin May, "the cross is broken. And I suppose there is no dance at all. Though there is still the beadle, stout and sour."

"Yes, since this old ballad was new, there must have been many and many a change in England and in Thorpe. In the last verse there is a fine strain of feeling."

"What! Is there more of it? Do let me hear it."

"I think it is good, very good. And there is in it a touch of that pathos which is wisdom. Think of it as being sung in a circle of neighbors, while they sit round the fire, which blazes up the chimney, a little higher than usual, on account of the day:—

'Martlemas shall come again,
Spite of wind and snow and rain
But many a strange thing must be done,
Many a cause be lost and won,
Many a fool must leave his pelf,
Many a worldling cheat himself,
And many a marvel come to pass,
Before return of Martlemas.'"

## XXXIV.

Percy Coke sat with his uncle in the parlor. The curtains were drawn. On the table the candles were set. And the uncle and the nephew sat, one on one side of the blazing fire, and the other on the other. After a long space of silence, Percy Coke said, "Uncle George, I must leave you to-morrow. For this I should be very sorry, only that you are now so very much better in health. But I shall return again soon."

"Where are you going to?"

"I am returning to Chelsea."

"What to do?"

"I want to write."

"And, Percy, if I may ask, what else do you want to do?"

"To — to —— Nothing."

"And cannot you here both write and do nothing?"

"Yes, sir. But I wish to be among my books."

"That I can quite understand. But could not you send to London for such volumes as you want? Indeed, rather than lose your company, I would myself have all your library brought here to Thorpe. And it can be done within four days. As to sharpening that pencil, — you cannot do it this evening. For I see your hand is very unsteady. And do you know that you have already cut away half of the pencil? You will excuse my remarking it, because it is the only one I have. You do not look well, Percy. You are not unwell, I hope; are you?"

"A little so; but it is only a very little."

"I hope we shall not both be ill together. And indeed, if you feel at all unwell, it would be very imprudent in you to make a journey to-morrow. If you feel ill, it would be more proper for you to remain here. For I suppose the air of London would do any thing rather than favor you."

"O, but, uncle George, if you will excuse me, I would much rather return to Chelsea for a little while."

"Because you expect that perhaps you may be ill; and so occasion us some trouble? Your sickness we should be sorry for. But trouble us you would not. For we should be only too happy to take all possible care of you."

"O, but if you please, uncle George, I must go to London for a few days."

"How can you be sure it will be only for a few days? And then, too, why should you go? What is the necessity? I suppose, Percy, you do not think it necessary to go to the metropolis for medical assistance, because you expect to be ill with some rare, recondite, difficult disease. There is medicine for your case accessible here, and a suitable physician, I have no doubt."

"For a month, only for a month; but, uncle, I must leave."

"And why must you? Cannot you tell me? To-night there is nothing you can speak of, to which I will not listen willingly. If it is any thing of philosophy, I will be as patient as though I understood it. If it is in the way of poetry, I am rather in the mood for it this evening. Or I will sympathize with you, if it is a matter of hatred of any body. Or if it is something more Christian than hate, and even the very reverse of it, then for that also I have some feeling, as being what better becomes your years and excellent temper. There now! And now you see that you can tell me nothing that will surprise me. And so, feeling as you do ——"

"I am therefore too poor to stay here."

"And yet the other day you were resolute to forego money-making and the habits of life, along which in cities men move and arrive at comfortable homes, and the dignities of alderman and mayor. And you seemed to think that out in the wilderness of life there would some raven bring food to a man, who, as having genius, has in him something of the prophet. But, Percy, it is not yet too late. By a fortunate chance, my place in the counting-house is yet open. And you shall fill it. Your leger will be neither Hebrew, nor Greek, nor German; but then, if you keep your attention well fixed upon it, whenever you do look up from the desk it will be into a future bright with prosperity, and happy with the wife who meets you every evening at the garden gate, and honorable by the high offices up to which you will be led for your worth."

"No more, no more! Do not say any thing more to me, uncle George. Because you would yourself hold it to be a weak, pitiful thing, if I were to forego the fixed purpose of years, and a call, as I have thought, almost divine, merely for this, — this feeling that is only of yesterday."

"But," said Mr. Coke, "I do not see why you

should forego either what you think is your duty, or what you feel would be your happiness. At present you are poor, but not miserably so. You are never likely to be rich. But yet, with the help of what little property you have, certainly you may reasonably hope, in time, even on your own way of life ——"

"But possibly that property may never get to be disencumbered. And even if any thing could be done with the entail upon it, yet you would yourself be unwilling to have it touched. But at the very best, what should I be to Mr. Pellet?"

"Be to him? What do you want to be to him? A partner? You would do better to succeed to me. Or perhaps you mean to be a teacher to him, for I should think he had never had one in any thing. Rival, — it is not that you mean?"

"Yes; and it is what I do not think I ought to be. And, indeed, I should disdain to try to make my poverty preferable to the comforts with which wealth can store a house."

"Percy, I think very highly of you. And that is exactly the way I should expect you to feel. And I must say that Pellet is a man of precisely that character with which many women would be pleased. He is not, perhaps, a person whom they would love, but yet one to be coveted. For certainly, Percy, you must know that a woman may be very beautiful, and be inspiration for poets, and yet herself not be poetical, but be a woman quite happy with small talk and pin-money. It is true that Tom Pellet does not talk much; but what he does say is certainly very small. A domestic man! He is as regular as the house-clock. I have met him three times in a day, and always he said, all in one breath, 'How do you do? Pretty well, thank you?' A very regular man! Now there are women of a temperament more equable than lively, for whom, in the order of nature, he is the very man for a husband. And so, Percy, in the course on which you have decided in your own mind there may be, not only honor, but also prudence. And no doubt, from what you know, you judge rightly in thinking that she ——"

"Do not, uncle," said Percy, "do not say it. Alice Heywood is no such woman. You do not know her, and so you do not understand her heart, veiled as it is by the modesty that is like a visible presence about her, and out of which her words come timidly. A soul of such purity, and gentleness, and affection, and varied thought! It has seemed to me as though with her mention of them all things grew beautiful; and as though with her graceful handling every object grew golden. And oh! with hearing her talk, I have had all the circumstances of life about me grow to feel sweet,—even disappointment and hardship. And with the sound of her voice I have had brought about me and over me the presence of a cathedral,—high and holy,—with solemn strains of music in it like worship."

"Then I should think that with her Mr. Pellet would feel uncomfortable, very often. And I do not think that she would herself be very happy in building up a temple of the Muses about a man, who has in his soul nothing of any one of the nine Muses, neither poetry, nor music, nor grace, nor eloquence, nor history, nor astronomy, nor tragedy."

"But neither am I worthy of her. And I feel it bitterly. Perhaps I might have been, if I had always been true to my knowledge of right. But I have not been. My follies and sins,—it seems as though they were calling after me from all along the course of my past life,—from the cities I lived in,—the schools I went to,—from one spot where I once quarrelled with a boy,—and from a wayward, passionate hour, when I was only five years old, but which I remember yet so distinctly and painfully. And these sins seem to call after me and challenge me for unworthiness. And almost they might forbid my happiness, even if there were no other hinderance in the way of it."

"A very proper feeling," said Mr. Coke. "For I have heard that Miss Alice is sensible and religious, — indeed, quite a right-minded young woman."

"So good, so cheerful! She dwells in such an atmosphere of purity. Always there are waiting on her, like ministering angels, such sweet, heavenly thoughts. And I do feel as though it might be wrong in me to seek to diminish her excellence by drawing her into sympathy with myself. For I am unworthy of her."

"No doubt. And so you are of any woman, — any good, true-hearted woman. And perhaps there is not a woman who would be worthy of you. And yet men and women are intended to be blessings to one another. And often they are. But when they are happy in one another, and more than happy, when they are blessed in one another, they are so, not simply from their being worthy of one another by nature, or from their thinking themselves so, but from there being about them a God by whose silent power hearts act on one another for good by unknown ways."

Here Mr. Coke seemed to forget the presence of his nephew, and sat apparently in earnest meditation. After a little time Percy said, "I had not expected so much sympathy from you, uncle. And really I was afraid I might have to hear from you something that might perhaps sound harsh to me. Because I suppose that you have always kept yourself free from any such trouble as this of mine. Yes, almost I was afraid of you. But sometimes how much we are mistaken in one another!"

"And how often! As you had intended to leave in the morning, I suppose you have taken your leave of the lady."

"I have of the house. For when I called at it, she was not in."

"And so you have left the lady to believe herself slighted, and to accept Tom Pellet, as being at least a man who knows his own mind, though it is rather little. Here have you been drawing the lady's thoughts to yourself ——"

"Never, never! Me! She has never had a thought of me, I am sure. Why, uncle, it is almost ridiculous to think ——"

"So it is. But I hope you do not think it is ridiculous in a lady to think at all, on any subject. You are possessed with the very spirit of what we will call tragedy, poetry, — no, we will call it music. You have been musical, and been playing your very best, and yet you have not made a tune, not one harmony, nothing which any body would recognize as music."

"Not a word —— "

"That will do. And now listen to me. You do not know yourself. But I know you. And it is fortunate for you that I do. I could show you your exact likeness. But I feel myself just now too weak to hold the mirror up to you. Proud, — proud! You are proud, and scarcely know it. Had Shylock by the merest trickery made a bargain with you, you would have been silent on it, and have folded your arms, and you would have let him cut away your flesh from your side, and even your heart, if he had preferred it. There is a pride, that is loud and oppressive, and it is very common. And there is another pride, that is very rare, but which by nature is silent and passive. And that is your pride. It has been mine, too, to my sorrow and hurt. And now do not let us be hasty. You shall not go to London for three days. But you shall go, to-morrow, to Manchester, where I have some business which needs your attention. You agree to this?"

"Yes, sir."

"In itself pride is a simple feeling, and may be known at once. But the finer are the elements of character which it pervades, the harder it becomes to understand. A man of a great heart, if he is proud, will often act as though perversely with the greatest simplicity, and will behave himself absurdly, out of the noblest considerations. Understood how should he be, when his actions are prompted by proud humility? — a quality which cannot even be described but in words of self-contradiction."

The last sentence Mr. Coke spoke as though to himself; his eye the while turning from his nephew to the fire, which no longer blazed up the chimney, but only glowed hot and red in the embers.

## XXXV.

"PRIDE, pride!" The day when the minister said that to Mr. Coke, there went through his mind a flash of light that was self-knowledge.

Pride, — of that, as a fault, he had never once suspected himself. For he was conscious of things which are inconsistent almost always with pride, — a heart tender as a child's, — a spirit self-accusing on the smallest fault, — a reverence for human nature even in the most ragged garb of a way-side beggar, — and a willingness to stand aside and let the unworthy pass on up to places of emolument and honor.

With the exception of one who was a spendthrift, and another who was only wise in his own eyes, the Cokes had all been men of the same type of character, and even of the same bodily look. The stature of Sir Humphrey in Drayton Church was the exact likeness of Mr. George.

And perhaps, from the time of Sir Humphrey, not one of these Cokes had ever known himself till now.

In the reign of Queen Elizabeth the family character was not uncongenial with the spirit of the times, and so was not without honor and some success in the world. But ever since the sixteenth century the Cokes had been declining. Yet they had sunk in the world probably without there ever having been a murmur from the lips of any one of them in seven generations.

Whenever any advantage had offered itself to one of them, almost always the impulse with him had been to self-inspection and self-suspicion. And several times one or other of them had behaved unwisely in their affairs, merely out of the fear of their possibly acting or being thought to act from unworthy motives. They abstained from things which they wanted to do, merely for fear of being thought to do them out of flattery. And they did some things which they did not wish to do, — things of no manner of propriety, — simply because they were afraid of being afraid of not doing them. Heroes who acted absurdly from the fear of being cowards! And often they had lost good friends, had ceased from communication with them, not from carelessness, but from fearing that themselves they must be, and must certainly be thought to be, unworthy of trust or kindness.

One day, as he sat thinking of his past life, Mr. Coke said to himself, "Pride, my besetting sin; pride! Would that I had come to this knowledge sooner! And yet would it have helped me? I hardly think it would; indeed, I am sure it would not. For I feel that I must still have acted the same, and been the same, — sensitive, fastidious, absurdly chivalric. No, no! I should not have walked in life any the more sensibly for having had a mirror in which to see myself, however steadily I had held it up to my face. Indeed, for a man of my subtle vice, the only true guidance is to see one's self in the eyes of a friend, and to have hold of a hand which one can press for love, and at times follow blindly."

## XXXVI.

Martin May had become intimate at Haslingden Hall. He found that Mr. Burleigh, the Justice, as he was called, was a man both credulous and suspicious, tyrannical and tender-hearted, very accessible and very kind to any person soliciting his help, and very fierce against every one offering him the least opposition. If a poor man with a starving family should pull up five or six turnips in a field, the Justice would commit him to prison for two months, and then maintain his family in his absence, and perhaps give the criminal a suit of clothes on his coming out of confinement. Every day, immediately after dinner, it was his custom to fill his glass, and then to drink as a toast, "England! And let them that do not like it leave it!"

His wife was a gentle, timid woman, and very beautiful. All her anxiety, and nearly all her thoughts, were for her two sons. Almost she feared to have any one speak to them. And very careful she was to keep them out of the way of her husband's acquaintance, who most of them were men ruddy with port-wine and fresh air.

For these two youths a tutor was wanted. And Martin May thought that it would be a good arrangement, if they could become the pupils of Percy Coke. After some inquiry and consultation, the Justice empowered Martin May to offer to Percy Coke very liberal terms for his acceptance, if he were willing to give instruction to two boys for four or five hours a day. This proposal Martin May called at Mr. Coke's to communicate, on the very day on which Percy had proposed to leave for London.

Percy Coke was glad to accept the proposal, because it insured him a maintenance and a residence at Thorpe. And he acquiesced in it all the more easily for the way in which the minister showed him the truth of Martin Luther's saying, that, in order to be a good theologian, it is well for a man first to be a schoolmaster.

"And," said the minister, "it is the truth; and it is so whether or not my reasons for the opinion are the same as Luther would himself have given. At one time I got together twenty, thirty, forty ignorant young men. And for a good while in an evening I taught them reading, writing, and other elementary knowledge. And I found that, with being earnest in teaching, my mind had come over it some very desirable effects as to simplicity and aptitude."

"I am glad to hear you say so," said Percy, without minding much what was said, for there seemed to open before him a beautiful vista into life; and he was thinking of three things like one, marriage, theology, and a tutorship.

The minister continued, "There are times, — I do not say they are my best or most hopeful seasons, — but there are times in which all my highest attempts feel like failures, and when I feel as though no one word of any sermon of mine had ever done any good. But of the people I taught their letters I can always think with some satisfaction; because, though persons may forget and do forget the very best discourses, they do not ever forget how to read. Next to that of a preacher, the office of a teacher of boys is the greatest and the best; so says Martin Luther. But there is one consideration which does not affect the schoolmaster, and which greatly abates for the clergyman his satisfaction with his office.

For, as the Reformer argues, it is hard to make old dogs tame, and old rogues upright; and yet at this task the preacher has to labor, and often labor in vain."

## XXXVII.

Mr. Coke sat by the fireside, and on a low chair near him, her hand on the arm of his chair, sat Louisa Lawton.

"I wish you many happy returns of the day," said the lady, as she looked up and smiled. "For do not you know that this is your birthday?"

"So it is. But I had forgotten it. Yet you, Louisa, you remember it still."

"Yes, every day for the last month I have remembered it was coming. And I thought I would be here for it. Ah, that smile! It was so like the way you used to smile when you came to Darley. And, George, you look so much better."

"Do I? And so do you. You are ten years younger than you were two months ago. You move, speak, and look now just as you used to, — that sweet, lively way. Ah, that glance of the eye! You have got it again."

"But, George, you do look so much better."

"It is because of you, and because my mind is easier than it was."

"O, but you are really better. Every body says so. And, George, you will be well soon. Or at least you will be so very much better. And oh! how happy that will be!"

"Louisa," said Mr. Coke solemnly, and he laid his hand on hers, "do not, — do not think so. I beg you not to think so. For really I am no better, — no better. I am happier than I was, but in health I am no better. I am no better, though with seeing you I am become very, very happy."

There was a pause, during which the tears streamed down the lady's face. At last she said, "O George, do not think so; do not think so! Do hope the best. I do not deserve to have you live; and I feel that I do not. But it cannot be that society is to lose you, — you so wise and good, — and just as you are becoming known. O, with your words there is so much wrong that ought to take a new shape, a new, happy shape, for the public! And so it cannot be, — it cannot be, George, that — that ——. But to-day is a dull, heavy day, and so you feel desponding. These last days of November are the worst that could be for you. And yet you look so much better even now than you did. And you will feel better soon, — when the weather becomes clearer, and the sun shines again. Ah, now you smile again, and I can see, and I am sure how much better you are. Do you remember it, George? I was thinking of it, yesterday, — that birthday of yours, when you were at Darley, and we went that ride between the rocks, when the leaves from out of the woods above were whirled along before us so curiously. Ah, little did I think then of that storm in which you would so soon be wrapped, and how I should remain standing apart from you in my quiet, comfortable home. O, to think that our happy prospects were all to end as they did!"

"Hush, hush!" said Mr. Coke, with a strange smile. "For, after all, our fortune has not been as hard as that of many other lovers of that time, and some of whom we knew, — some who were married and were then at once parted by death, — some who were quite mistaken in one another, — some who found they could love only as long as they were prosperous, — and some who soon found their partners grow tedious."

"O George, you pain me, talking so. For," said the lady in a tone of tender conviction, "you know our love never, never could ——"

"Hush, Louisa! For it is selfishness in me to let you talk thus. It is a sweet, sweet temptation. But yet, Louisa, it is wrong in me to let my heart be pleased with your affectionate words. Because never, never can love, for me, be any thing else than anxiety, and very soon it must be mere pain."

"Those are cruel words, George, very cruel," said the lady, with a trembling voice. "I know you do not mean them so; but they are. O, you must unsay them, dear George. And the truest, highest love, — is not it always thoughtful, and therefore always more or less anxious?"

"But this love against the gates of the grave," said Mr. Coke, "this unfortunate love ——"

"Is better than never to have loved at all. O, unsay those words; because they will be very hard for me to think of. Since what now is there left me in this world? Of all the sweetness of ten years ago, when my mother folded me to her bosom, because I was so happy that I wept; and when my father's voice was loud and merry in the garden and the field; and when you used to come to Darley Dale, making every body feel as though it were a holiday time, — of it all, what is there remaining to me, but this long, dear — this — this ——"

"This unfortunate affection, which I should try to have you forget, were I as unselfish as I ought to be."

"To the — the — the last, — always, I must love; and you must let me. Or else how will it be, if you do not. How will it be with me, if my life be emptied of its meaning? For what does it mean? It means how sweet, heavenly sweet, love may be even in human hearts, — how precious a possession it is, even when it is become a remembrance only, — and how even a recollection of frustrated love may for years and years be like a lamp in a tomb, sad, but undying."

"Sad, and therefore what ought not to be allowed to be undying," said Mr. Coke, and took in his the hand of the lady.

"And, besides, George, I have learned from you to believe that it is not merely as being something delightful in a happy, earthly home, that God lets rise in us this sweet affection, but also that by it our hearts may be strengthened with courage for the grave, and with hope for the future beyond it. And, indeed, I have myself experienced something of this. Ah, yes, those old, sweet remembrances, — they were long the strength on which I lived, unfortunate, but not utterly unhappy. But those tears, — why those tears?"

"Not for any thing of pain, love, but only for this great happiness, which I do not deserve."

"Then you will not say again as though you would rather — rather — rather not have me speak my love. You will not speak so again?"

"No; not again, Louisa, never again."

"It is this weather which is so much against you. And you are weak with the want of fresh air. Though indeed you are better than you were, much; for you look much better. And now, George, do think yourself so, for my sake. Very soon these foggy days will be over; and then it will be Christmas; and then the days will lengthen; and then soon it will be spring and be warm. And you will get strong then; I am sure you will."

"Why, all that is next year, Louisa. And it is a long while to next summer. And in the mean time, you must help me to pray to God that his will may be done. And cannot we learn to feel that will so holy and good, so trustworthy, as being God's own, so as that we should long towards it, and bow to it devoutly and gladly, in whatever shape it comes and shows itself?"

"We will hope, we will trust we may; but O, dear George ——"

"Hush! hear me. If I were in my last sleep,

lying in a tomb, and angels should come and wake me up, and then leave it to me either to return to health and strength and you, on my own wish, or to have God decide for me for the best, I do believe I should lie down, and shut my eyes, and fold my hands, and say, 'God's will be done.' And what I should pray in the darkness of the grave, — ought it not to be my prayer and your prayer, — our prayer in the darkness of human life? To pray God to do his will, — heartily to pray him that, after having overcome a craving of our own will, — this is a great, blessed thing; and the chance, the opportunity of doing it, is a great privilege allowed me And so I feel it. And, Louisa, of my life there is many a recollection which I would gladly forget. But the things I could wish to forget I cannot forget. But yet I feel as though the pain of them would cease in my heart, if only my soul could shape itself so as to show itself perfectly reconciled to God, — afflicted of God, yet trusting him, resigned to him, loving him. And, Louisa, toward feeling as I ought your words will help me much, for they so soothe, and purify, and encourage me."

The lady held Mr. Coke's hand, and, bowing her forehead on to it, she wept and sobbed. It grew dusk. And when the lady had become calm again Mr. Coke said, " Whether we smile or weep, see now how time goes on. We weep, and it grows dark; and had we been laughing, still it would have grown dark, only perhaps a little faster. For, ah! there is on us and about us a power which is influence over us, — change, impulse, and authority, — gloom and pleasure, day and night, an answer to prayer, and wisdom that is infinite. And we, Louisa, — if we have not had our happiness, it has not been because we have failed of it, but because we have been drawn to forego it by this power which we call divine, and which we worship. Though we will not think of God as being careless of the love which we human creatures feel for one another. Yours and mine, — our love for one another, — this growth of our hearts at their best may have been unfortunate, but yet I believe in this world there is nothing more beautiful than it is, — not even to that omnipresent eye which evermore has open to it the workings of the highest intellects, and the interiors of solemn cathedrals, and the recesses of vast forests, and the secret depths of the earth."

" Ah, that is as you used to talk. Do not you remember the evening when we sat on the rock at Matlock, with the river running below ? "

"O the memories we have in common, — remembrances of long ago, and yet sweet and fresh as growing flowers!"

"O George, I like to hear you speak so!"

"And O the magical power of your name on me now so long, and of mine on you! Is not it so?"

"George!"

"And with loving one another, O the way our souls towered up, high above the world and all meanness! And with knowing one another's souls, O the spiritual way life felt and nature! And because of its being what it is, — this love of ours, — there is more in it than what will cease at the grave. Mine, Louisa, you are mine, as you used to say, — mine for ever."

## XXXVIII.

On the afternoon of the shortest day, in the porch of St. John's Church, there was distributed what was called St. Thomas's dole, — a yearly gift of bread to the poor, bequeathed by some good Catholic of the fourteenth century. On a table were piled up loaves of bread. And beside the table stood the two church-wardens. They were both of them corpulent and ruddy, and nearly seventy years of age. One of them incessantly took snuff from a gold box, which he held open in his hand. And the other often twirled about a great bunch of seals, which hung suspended from his watch.

Outside the porch, in the churchyard, stood the poor people, — old men ragged, and some of them deaf, and some of them blind, — old women dressed in scarlet cloaks, and very clamorous for their turns, — and some young women, looking pale and worn, though clean. And on the steps of the porch, with a club-stick in his hand, stood the bellman, looking fierce and active.

Martin May at this time happened to be crossing the Market-place: and seeing the crowd, he went up to the church, and very officiously was ushered into the porch by the bellman. Among the last of the poor admitted inside the porch was a young woman of a very pretty, modest look, and with a child in her arms.

"You here!" cried one of the wardens. "There is nothing for you. Go away. I saw that Tom Doolittle of yours down in my pasture. He was setting snares for rabbits. I know him. And I only wish I could have caught him. And then you to come here, with that child in your arms! Shame on you!"

The young woman never answered a word; but went out of the porch at once. Martin May followed her a few steps, and saw that the tears were rolling fast down her cheeks, and dropping on her baby.

"What does this mean?" said Martin May to her. "You seem very poor. So how is it that you have not a loaf like the others?"

"Please, sir, it is because I am not married," said the young woman, and hung down her head and blushed.

"Not married! And yet you —— Why, how is this?"

"It is because we are so poor. But we have always been faithful to one another. Of that I am very sure. And twice Thomas has paid to have the banns of marriage put up in the church. And the first time, all the while till the notice was out, we had not the rest of the money to be married with. And so we lost what had been paid to the clerk. And so we shall again. Because, last October, Thomas paid two shillings to have the banns published in the church again. And next Friday is the last day that we can be married on that notice. And now again we have not got the rest of the money for the parson. O dear, O dear! I know it is very wrong. But what can we do, — we poor people? It costs so much money to be married; and we cannot even buy bread."

"Well now, I will promise you that, if you will go to Mr. Lingard, he will marry you for nothing."

"Please, sir, my mother was married in this church."

"And do you attend this church?"

"O, sir, we poor people cannot come to church. We have not got clothes fit for church. And then, besides, there is always something to keep us poor women at home. But my mother used to come sometimes, and always on Good Friday."

"And Mr. Doolittle, does he come to church?"

"O, no, sir! He says he will come here with me once, to be married, and be brought here when he is dead. And that is all that he will ever come, he says. For he is so angry at losing twice over the money which he has paid for having the banns put up. And please, sir, I tell him that he ought not to talk so. But it all comes of his keeping company with Humphrey Sharples."

"Does Doctor Scoresby know that he has been paid twice over for publishing your banns?"

"Please, sir, I cannot tell."

"Now I have no doubt that what you have told me is quite correct. And if it is, you will go, this evening, to John Kittringham. Do you know him?"

"Yes, sir. He is the sexton at the Presbyterian Chapel. And he lives just round the corner, there. But, sir, he does not know me, — not at all."

"Never mind that. Do you call at his house this evening. And he will give you the money for you to be married to-morrow morning. And, besides, he will give you half a crown for a Christmas dinner."

The young woman went away, thinking not much of the joys of marriage, but feeling cheered with the hope, that next morning she should emerge from under a cloud of shame.

"Sir," said the bellman, "it is all of no use to give money to that kind of people. She will be just as poor to-morrow morning."

"And yet you have been giving away all those loaves!"

"O, that is a different thing. That is the law."

"I understand that this bread was left to the poor in Catholic times."

"Very likely. And what a trouble it is, every year, for us parish officers! A strange people those Catholics were, — a people of no manner of reason, as I have read."

Leaving the bellman at the church door, Martin May walked down Church Street. And every here and there he noticed signs of the approaching Christmas, — at the butchers' shops unusually fat beef, decorated with laurel, — and at the grocers' a great display of plums and currants and other fruits. And at the gate of the almshouses he saw a man carrying in a great holly-bush, covered with scarlet berries.

Martin May had never yet seen the inside of the almshouses. And so he followed the man who was carrying in the tokens of Christmas. At the almshouses he did not find any thing remarkable anywhere except in the chapel, where there was an old, very old picture. It was the portrait of a woman ghastly pale, beautiful by nature, but from some cause looking miserable, utterly and hopelessly. Martin May sat down upon a bench and gazed up at the picture. Almost he wondered that that look of agony never relaxed. And he fancied that possibly he might even have been drawn into such sympathy with the pictured woe, as to have shrieked at the sight of it, only that the womanly sufferer herself looked so calm and resolute with her misery.

When he left and went up the street, he felt as though he had just come away from a scene of suffering, — some sudden discovery of treachery, — some death-bed, where a young wife has suddenly known herself a widow. And he thought how strange it was that such a picture should be in such a place, — and how wonderful it was that that painted agony should be lasting on, age after age, making spectators fear how wretched perhaps they themselves might sometimes become. And while he was thinking of this, he remembered the young woman by the church porch. And he was glad of having met her, and been her timely helper. But still that face! He could not forget it; though it did not pain him to recollect. For now that he was away from it, he found that he remembered it more and more as an expression of calmness in agony, — as an intimation of how the soul is stronger than grief, — any grief.

And as he went on up the street towards the Parsonage, he said to himself, "A procession from the cradle to the grave, — a journey, during which, earlier or later, there is a cross laid upon every one, — that is what life is. A pilgrim after Adam and Eve, or more exactly after Adam, when perhaps Eve was dead, — and more hopefully, and in a diviner way, a follower after Christ, — that is what I am!" And thinking so, he felt that he was become more resigned than once he had ever hoped to be.

Martin May said to the minister, "It seems to me, that these Christmas customs and the practices in celebration of the new year have blended in them very singularly things of Druidical and Roman and Christian origin."

On his saying this, the minister laid open before him a volume, in which he read these words of a sermon by St. Ambrose: — "The order of eternal life is one thing, and the recklessness of temporal passions is another thing. How can you religiously observe the festival of the manifestation of our Lord, when you devoutly celebrate the Calends? For Janus was a man, the founder of a city, now called Janiculum, in whose honor the Calends of January were instituted by the Gentiles. And he sins who pays divine honor to a dead man. Brethren, let us shun every festivity of the Gentiles, that when they feast we may fast. And in like manner let us avoid all conversation with the Jews, which is a great pollution."

"How oddly this reads!" said Martin May.

"Yes," answered the minister, "with reading it, almost I can fancy it is the end of the fourth century, and that I am at Milan, standing beneath the pulpit while Ambrose preaches, and that he is making me afraid that Christianity will certainly be more and more corrupted by Paganism."

"St. Ambrose! do you esteem him much as a writer?"

"No: nor do I know him much. He was often and successfully opposed to men, whom perhaps I should have judged more nearly right than himself. But I believe that, in his place and age, and in such way as he thought was best, he lived and worked like a true man."

"O these old, old words!"

"Yes, how some men's voices keep echoing round and round the world with undying power! Lasting on, from there being in them a something immortal from the soul which spoke them! So at least I love to think."

## XXXIX.

On Christmas eve, in the kitchen at the Dell, Martin May was pleased by seeing the servants hang from the ceiling a bough of mistletoe, — an evergreen of white berries, which grows parasitically out of the side of some tree. And he thought of how the Druids used to go into the woods, in solemn procession, to gather the mistletoe with a golden knife. And he remembered that at York the Minster stands on the site of some Druidical structure, and that he had read somewhere, that even in the last century there used to be a procession to carry mistletoe to the cathedral; after which at Monk-bar, Mickle-gate-bar, and the other gates of the city, there was proclaimed a temporary liberty and pardon for all sorts of low and dissipated persons.

At seven o'clock there was placed on the fire a great log of wood, called a Yule-clog. And then there were lighted four tall candles, of double the usual length. At supper-time there was placed on the table a great bowl of what was called furmety, — a condiment probably of Roman origin, and made of milk, currants, and wheat.

After Martin May had gone to bed and to sleep, he was suddenly awoke by a band of musicians, called the waits, who played a tune in front of the house, and then went away. Soon afterwards he had a miserable dream of two immense black gates which reached up to the sky, and which were visible in the dark, they were so black. And from these gates he could not turn away; for his eyes were drawn to them quite irresistibly. At last, without their having opened, it seemed as though there had come through them, and were coming toward him, two long, fiery serpents, gliding together, one on each side of a path. At this he awoke in a fright: and then he heard two boys underneath his window, finishing a Christmas carol: —

"As it fell out, upon a day,
  Rich Dives sickened and died;
There came two serpents out of hell,
  His soul therein to guide.

"Rise up, rise up, brother Dives,
  And come along with me;

For you have a place provided in hell,
To sit on a serpent's knee."

Again and again, during the night, he was awakened by the carol-singers. And neither time was he as well pleased as the first. But the last time he awoke was just at the dawn. And he said to himself, "This, then, is Christmas Day!" And he felt as though, in some manner, he ought to be more happy than he was. Then suddenly he was aware of a very sweet voice, that of a young woman, singing a very ancient carol: —

"He neither shall be born
In housen nor in hall,
Nor in the place of paradise,
But in an ox's stall.

"He neither shall be rocked
In silver nor in gold;
But in a wooden cradle,
That rocks on the mould.

"He neither shall be clothed
In purple nor in pall;
But all in fair linen,
As are babies all."

On going down stairs, he found that every room was decorated with holly and ivy. And on going out of doors, he heard from Thorpe the bells ringing a merry peal, with their six iron tongues.

It was a bright, clear morning, and every thing was white with frost. About the house the sparrows were thick; and in the garden the robin was singing from tree to tree. Martin May now felt the happiness of the day; and, looking up on high, he thought there might even be joy in heaven over the joy of earth. And he repeated to himself these lines from Milton's Hymn on the Nativity:—

"Ring out, ye crystal spheres,
Once bless our human ears,
If ye have power to touch our senses so;
And let your silver chime
Move in melodious time,
And let the bass of Heaven's deep organ blow."

On his way to attend divine service at the chapel, he supposed that at least a hundred persons wished him a merry Christmas. He saw walking before him Percy Coke and Alice Heywood. In his eyes they moved together as though with a glory round them. He walked fast to overtake them. And then he suddenly stood still, and wondered at himself. Yes! It was so. He was really hastening to rejoice with the joyful. He drew a long breath, and it became a thanksgiving to God. For he felt that now he was no longer a man woebegone, and likely to be useless. And he said, "That dear saint in heaven! Still she draws all my thoughts and feelings towards her. But this void by my side, — this shadow that walks with me, — it is no longer painful. And now almost I can love to feel it, as being a memorial of her." And then he thought of his home in America. And he felt himself attracted towards it. And almost he wondered at how much he now longed for the sight of what he had left, abandoned, hastened from, in tears and wretchedness.

He felt light of heart, and even joyous. He saw a lark rise from the ground, and he heard it singing its happy, triumphant song, even when it had soared out of sight. And then he remembered the despondent lines of the Minnesinger, which he had repeated to the minister, by the side of the water, when the thrush was singing before the coming of the storm. And he felt that now he was another man than he was. And as he walked on towards the chapel, he thought of what was once a custom at Rheims. For on Christmas morning, in the cathedral of that city, birds were let loose out of a cage, as emblems of what Christ does for the soul, in freeing its hopes and aspirations from imprisonment by despair and sin.

## XL.

The day after Christmas Day, in the afternoon, there drew up before Mrs. Gentle's house a private carriage, with a coachman in a gorgeous livery on the box, and with a footman behind, also in livery. There stepped from the carriage a tall gentleman of about forty years of age. In manner he was quick and conceited. And his limbs seemed to hang loosely in their sockets. He looked at the house contemptuously, and then said, partly at the gate, and partly as he walked up the alley: "Is this the house, John? Are you sure you are right? Poor place for a man like Coke! Ah, ah! This comes of being a Radical, and making speeches to the people. But clever as he thought himself, he was often a great fool, — a great fool. There was Lord Grandeaux, who thought to make something of him, and so invited him to dinner. But he would not go. Refused a lord! And now see what comes of it!"

With some little difficulty Mrs. Gentle consented to let the gentleman see Mr. Coke, who had been growing worse for the last few days, and was now lying on a sofa in the parlor.

"Ah," said the gentleman, "you do not know me. Your room is rather dark. Do not you know me? Do not you know me?"

"Yes," said Mr. Coke, very deliberately. "You are Mr. Judas, — I beg your pardon. You are Mr. Jude Bamforth."

"Now I will wager any money you never expected to see me this afternoon. But I am come."

"I see you are. Take a seat. And excuse my rising. And because I am ill, I shall be glad if you will be brief in whatever you want to say."

"Why, Coke, you are always ill. At least you have always looked so this long while. But what I want to say is this. My wife knows of —— Clever woman, my wife! But you know her."

"No, I do not. I did not know you were married."

"Not know it! Why, I married Peggy Grey. You remember, Coke, how, ten years ago, our house got the better of you. But Peggy says you were not treated quite fairly. But you know in the way of trade, Coke ——"

"It was not in the way of trade."

"Not in the way of trade! Why, what else could it have been?"

"It was in the way of false witness and deliberate swindling."

"Ah, well, well, trade is trade. And, after all, if you are in trade you have got to trade."

"Sir, if there is any sense of justice in you, or any religion ——"

"Religion! That is the matter exactly. You see, I married Peggy Grey. And we set up our carriage. And so Peggy said, to be respectable, I ought to go to church. So we took a pew. And I pay twenty pounds a year for it, in Doctor Thunderby's church. Did you ever hear him, Coke? O, to hear him preach on hell is enough to make any man religious! I never knew what a sinner I was till I heard him. Desperate sinners we all are, Coke, — horrid sinners, — deserving hell for any day's work, — ay, or any minute's, — ay, and even for being alive, as Doctor Thunderby says."

"Even for your being alive, Mr. Bamforth! I am sure myself that I never thought it of you. But if you believe it, I have no reason to doubt it of you. And now, again, may I ask you why I have the honor — the interruption — the circumstance of a visit from you?"

"At our church there is vital religion preached; and where we sit in our pew ——"

"Mr. Bamforth, I am very ill. And in ten minutes I shall go to my bedchamber. If the subject be cotton, you can talk to the point directly. Now try to do so on your present business; and let me know it at once. For what is it to me, your going to church in a carriage, and your sitting in a pew at a rent of twenty pounds a year?"

"Well, then, Peggy cannot be easy till I have got a receipt from you for five hundred pounds. Ten years ago in our house my share was one eighth. It was not more, — not a fraction, not a penny more. I can prove it from the books, any time, anywhere, to any body. I say, Coke, my share in our house ten years ago was an eighth, and no more. But if it had not been for you, our house would have lost four thousand pounds by that Yorkshireman. However, he chose to fail in your debt, and not in ours. And so there was a saving to me of five hundred pounds."

"And you and your partners vouched to me for that man's solvency and honor! And when I had trusted him, on your representations, then you had him pay you with my goods."

"Well, Coke, it was rather a close business.

But they were hard times just then, very hard. Why, if we could not have got our debt out of that Yorkshireman, we must have failed. And when it comes to that, — whether I shall fail or you shall fail, — why, then, trade is trade. But Peggy is not easy about it. You must know her, for she says that she used often to be with the landlady of the house where you lodged. And since we have been to Doctor Thunderby's often on a Sunday night, she has talked about you. But a month ago, on a Monday, she mentioned our old affair with you; and when I told her that I had heard from Mr. May that you were very ill, she said that it would never do for you to die with me in your debt. Debt! But women cannot understand matters. Just as though you would not have had the money by law, if I had owed you a debt! But she says she does not feel easy on the matter. And for a month she has been asking, what is five hundred pounds to me."

"And it is not much, I suppose, Mr. Bamforth. Your house now has four mills."

"Four mills, six warehouses, and three thousand five hundred hands in employ. Energy, business energy does it all. Nothing like it in this world! Every man to his department! I have mine; Joe has his; and Simpkins his. We employ thirty clerks. Think of that, Coke. Bamforth, Simpkins and Co., — great house, very great house! What a cough you have got! Why do not you take a box of pills, — those pills with the odd name?"

Here Mr. Bamforth rose and walked up and down the room, and continued, "Next year we shall be the largest house in Lancashire. Energy, energy, — that is our way. There comes to me a man to ask me to subscribe to a prison-reformation society. But I soon let him know he was not going to have a moment from me, nor any body else in our employ. A man with an instant to waste in our warehouse, — I would discharge him in a minute."

"But prison reform, I should have thought you would have been interested in that."

"I? Not I! What have I to do with a prison? What are prisons to me? No matter of mine. All the week I have no time for any thing but business. And on the Sabbath it is all religion. Three times a day we attend service, and travel four miles every time. Energy, energy! That is what does it! It is ——"

"Mr. Bamforth, I am very ill. Will you sit down, and, whatever your business is, prepare to transact it?"

"O, you want the check! Pen and ink! O, there they are, I see. And you will give me a receipt. There! That is what you will sign, Coke."

"When I have the money, I will."

"Sharp man, Coke, sharp man! Well, now, there is the money, and there is the receipt."

"But this receipt is for five hundred pounds, and interest thereon."

"Yes, that is what Peggy says I must bring her."

"But you have only given me a check for five hundred pounds."

"Well, will not that do for you?"

"Not if I am to say that I have had the interest on it besides."

"O, but you know that I am not obliged to pay you any money at all."

"Nor am I obliged to receive it at all." And so saying, Mr. Coke pushed from him the receipt unsigned, and the bank-check which had been given him.

"Well, now, if I pay you the interest, it shall be at the rate of three per cent., the same as in the government stocks. The three per cents, — no safer investment in the world!"

"And has my money been a safe investment with you?"

"No better house than ours in Manchester! None that can get a loan from the banks sooner than we!"

"And when you borrow at five per cent., you can make twenty per cent. profit."

"We can if any body can. Energy, energy,— it is that that does it. Well, there is a check for six hundred and seventy-five pounds. And now give me the receipt. There! And now Peggy will be satisfied. And you are satisfied, Coke. Are you not? Now it is all clear between us, is not it? Say so, say so."

"I cannot say so, and I will not say so, for I do not think so."

"O, yes, you do. Yes, you do. It is all clear you know, between us now. Come, say so."

"I shall not say so. I should be wronging you, helping to falsify your conscience if I did say so. For it is not all clear between us. You have never acknowledged the treachery of your conduct towards me. And even now, in making restitution for your fraud, you defraud me again, with giving me three per cent. for interest, when legal interest is at the rate of five per cent. Your conduct now is better than I should ever have expected from you. But I will not say that you are perfectly honest with me, or that I think you stand innocent towards me: for I do not think you do."

"Come, Coke, you have got my money——"

"Your money, Mr. Bamforth! It is my own, and a very small part of what you ought to see restored to me. But, as I have already said, I am better satisfied——"

"Ah, well, well, you are satisfied, quite satisfied."

"This afternoon, Mr. Bamforth——"

"Satisfied this afternoon! And now I will tell Peggy. For that is all she wants. Fine woman, clever woman! Though when she wants a thing done, right or wrong, she will have it done. She is what I am in trade. It is energy, energy does it. Nothing like energy, Coke! Ah, there is my carriage! First-rate article, built by Leader in Long-acre! There is some style in that. See how it hangs! That is Peggy's taste. I say, Coke, get married when you get well."

"I am glad, Mr. Bamforth, there has been so much good for you in marriage."

"O, ay, Coke, get married. It is all very well for clerks and junior partners to live about in lodgings, and sport about on Sundays. But at our years, and when a man has got property to answer for, it is time for him to settle in the world, and to get religion, — vital religion."

"But does not it interfere with trade?"

"What! religion? Not at all! not at all! I never attend any week-day services. Not I! I am principled against them. Sunday is the Sabbath. And Monday is for business. And besides twenty pounds a year for a pew, and twenty pounds for this, that, and the other, how could I get it all to pay it, but for business on Monday and Tuesday, and every hour all the week, and system and energy? Energy, energy, — it will do any thing in this world."

"Especially with some men, and when it is not restrained by fears, — when it is not restricted by ——"

"Restricted energy is nothing, — nothing. Let me see my object, and go straight for it, and get it. That is energy, Coke, my energy. And I say there is nothing like it for a man. It is character, and business, and good profits, and a fortune perhaps in five years."

"And perhaps a loss of his spirit for ever," said Mr. Coke, solemnly.

"Why, a man gets worn out with it. But still energy is energy, and there is nothing like it."

Mr. Bamforth had left the house, when Mr.

Coke had him called back, and on his entering the room, Mr. Coke said to him, " I want to say to you one thing more on this matter between us."

" No more money, Coke! No more money! I cannot afford it. I say, I cannot afford it. And you know there is not one of my old partners who has done as much for you as I have. Is there now? And besides, money is scarce now, very scarce. Six hundred and seventy-five pounds! Think of that, Coke."

" I do think of it. And it is a great sum as coming from you. But possibly the time may come, when you will think it a little thing. And perhaps when I am dead, you will be desirous to make me perfect restitution. And you will not be able to have me answer you, when you can only come to my grave to talk with me. Perhaps some time you will wish that you had acknowledged your fraud upon me, — perhaps even wish this check had been for a larger amount. It may happen that you may desire my entire forgiveness, when I shall not be here to give it you. And so, against you want it, I now give it you freely, on condition that you will be generous with some worthy man, up to the amount of what more money you may owe me. And if it ever should happen to you to lose your fortune, then think at that time that you are not only forgiven, but pitied. Good by, Bamforth."

Mr. Bamforth, with his hand in his pocket, stood hesitating for a moment whether or not to enlarge the amount of the check which he had given. But something of pride rose up in his mind to hinder him. And when Mr. Coke ceased speaking, he left the room, and as he went to his coach he wiped away a tear, and said, "A queer fellow, that Coke, — a queer fellow! And so he always was. But however, Peggy will be glad with what I have done. Well, I have done that much, at least. I have done that much. And I can do more, if I like, — some time when I like. Cannot I? For who is there to hinder me? what is to hinder me?"

## XLI.

Mr. Coke told the minister of Mr. Bamforth's visit, though not of quite all that had passed at it, and said, "His visit was very painful to me, while it lasted, but yet I find it pleasant to remember. It is not that the money pleases me much; nor is it that I was pleased with either his face or his talk; and yet in some way, from that interview with him, I feel myself more cheerful, and even stronger for death. But, Mr. Lingard, I do not know why I should."

"Naturally, in any one, in any way, goodness cheers us. But besides that, every righteous action makes us sensible of the moral order of the universe. Jude Bamforth returned you that money; and all the more unlikely he was to have done so, all the more must his manner and tone have made you feel the motives which were acting upon him, — fear of the invisible that appalled him, and the desire to be right with God that drew him."

"Yes, probably, that is to say, perhaps; for I am not sure that he knew what his motives were. But there is a great truth in what you were saying, I think; and perhaps it may be the real account of what I feel."

"An act of liking may involve in it no more than two persons. But it is not so with an act of justice; because in that there are concerned, not merely the two persons between whom the justice is done, but also God, whose watchful eye is the sanction of it. When a man acts honestly, one feels that he does so because of his having some feeling of justice and judgment, which are unearthly things, and are the foundations of God's throne. Any noble thing I witness, — every strenuous act of honesty, every instance of great love, every holy struggle, — makes me thrill with a spirit that is consciously immortal."

"That is worth thinking of, Mr. Lingard."

"Every thing which exceeds the righteousness of the Scribes and Pharisees, every truly righteous deed, is a something not of the world, — not of this mere world of dust, earth and food and day and night; and therefore it is a prophecy and a testimony of the infinite, — a something with the sound of which on earth one feels that even the heavens may echo."

"The nearer I approach the next world," said Mr. Coke, "the more do I find myself dying to this world. I do not merely mean dying to its business, for which I have no longer any head, — nor dying to its wide fields and steep hill-sides, for which I have no longer any feet, — nor dying to its fruits, nutritious and luscious, for which I have no longer any appetite, — nor dying to its weather, clear and calm one day, and stormy another, for which I have now little interest. But I mean that I am dying daily more and more to many a recollection and purpose of my own past life. Six months ago it was a pleasure to me to recollect things in which now I have no interest, — the various steps by which I accomplished some political object, — the statements, the arguments, the retorts, by which I vanquished an opponent, — scenes of which I have been a witness in the city, collisions between the military and the people, and a wicked man on a public platform, white with the sudden detection of his wide and cruel machinations, — journeys which I have made in France, and Scotland, and Ireland, — mountains, from whose tops I have looked on cities lying like specks upon the plains below, —

the look and the terror of a storm at sea, — and books which I have read, and by which one is permitted to be a safe witness of bloody revolutions, a joyous guest at marriage-feasts, a fellow-traveller with Humboldt, a fellow-student with Niebuhr, a companion with great poets, in their seasons of high rapture, and a spectator of what is most comic and whatever is most tragic in the life together of us men. But now they do not stir me at all, —things which once so moved me to admiration and laughter and curiosity, and wonder and terror and indignation."

"But do not you find, Mr. Coke, that there are some things which you remember now more vividly than you used to do?"

"Yes, there are so. Now, when I think of the past, the recollections which rise before me most vividly are of such incidents as I felt tenderly, — my mother in the garden, calling me to walk with her, — the young amazement with which my soul first woke up to the knowledge of God, by my happening once to discover my grandfather praying in secret, — and the times of earnest, quiet conversation which I had with my betrothed in winter by the fireside, and in summer among the trees."

"Your heart shall live for ever, says the Psalmist. Those are beautiful words at all times, but against death they must sound and feel so sweet as well as true. The acclamations of a vast multitude may not reach through the ear of a dying man; and he may be deaf to the echoes of his fame reverberating about him; and yet there may be living on in his heart, distinctly audible to his inward ear, the whispers of his mother's love."

"More and more real life feels against death," said Mr. Coke.

"Making one feel," said the minister, "that really the tomb is the House of the Living, as the Jews call it."

"House of the Living! A happy phrase! But with death's hand upon his shoulder, O, what things a man could say and write, if only he were strong enough."

The minister leaned back in his chair, as was almost always his custom when he was about to make a quotation; and then he said: "In one of the dialogues of Plato, an old man remarks to Socrates, 'Know this well, that, when any one thinks himself near death, he fears and reflects about things which had never occurred to him before.' But how different from this old man's sentiment must have been the feeling of St. Theresa, who said that all her hope was in death, and that she was dying of regret that she could not die."

"But were those words of hers uttered when she was old?"

"I think not."

"And myself I should have been sure not," said Mr. Coke.

"No, they were not spoken in any nearness to death, but were written by her in a little book which she published. Truer to nature, perhaps, were the words of Mère Angelique on her deathbed, when she told the weeping nuns, that, though she had had death in her mind for more than fifty years, yet all her serious thoughts had been nothing to the unspeakable awfulness of what she then felt. For, said she, as the soul stands between time and eternity, ready to ascend to God, the earth itself sinks and dwindles into a mere speck."

"How true that is, Mr. Lingard, how true that is! For, as I was telling you just now, it is sunk away from about me, so much of what was once my world. The words of those who have gone through that gate of death at which I am now waiting, — they have such an interest for me now, tender, deep, and of a kind such as I have never felt before. Fellow-creatures men were to me while I was strong and busy, but now they are my fellow-pilgrims; and in the gateway of death we are so near one another."

"A gateway, a passage, — what a universal emblem of death that is! Says a French writer, 'Natural death is only a passage from God to God, from one paradise to another.' And one who is a great authority on the significance of Catholic emblems writes in one of his works, that in death we pass from one Church to another, from the Church Militant to the Church Triumphant."

"A passage dark, very dark, though with a daystar shining through it! A dark, dark gateway! And we meet at it, — children, youths, and patriarchs; and all of us of an age, in some sense. There are reasons for which I could wish to continue to live; but they are not for myself, I think. Yet this indifference about living is not a want of perception as to the uses of life, I hope."

"O, no, I do not think it is. The other day I met with a curious quotation from Henry Suso, in which he remarks that our blessed Saviour chose not to protract his life beyond its flower; while it was an Antipope who prolonged the period of what was his usurpation beyond the years of St. Peter."

"I like that. And I like that evidence of self-possession amid strange experiences, which is betokened by the blending together of the solemn and the humorous, in the manner of some of the last words of Socrates. How calm he was while dying, even in his heathen darkness! But some of us Christians have known more than he did only to trust less. However, I do not wonder at the misgivings in death to which some men have confessed. For already one feels how surely the soul will cease living in many a worldly direction; while of how it will live beyond death there is so little to be known, there is so very little revealed. Myself I do not feel this to be any manner of trouble. But I suppose, in the expectation of death, there have been persons who have been troubled ——"

"Because," said the minister, "because they did not consider, like Montaigne, that we all come to death as apprentices, and not as masters; and because, also, they did not reason like Luther. For one day, at his table, the Reformer said that he understood but little of what the manner of the next life would be, just in the same way as he little knew how he should afterwards eat and drink and live, while he was sucking upon his mother's breasts."

## XLII.

At the Parsonage, on the last day of the year, in the evening, there sat round the fire in the study Martin May, Percy Coke, and the minister.

"Now I am where the Pilgrims went from,— some of them. And I shall be where they went to, in a month, I hope."

"At the ground they went to," said Percy Coke. "But since their landing on it the soil has become the foundation of cities, and institutions, and things of immortal promise. And the England from which they emigrated,— how changed that is!"

"It is, and it is not; both. A Pilgrim Father would not find much which he would recognize, if he should walk about London, grown almost to be a kingdom in itself; or if he could see Liverpool, bordered now with a forest of masts, instead of shallow water almost stagnant; or if he should be shown a cotton-mill, or be taken into some iron-works, or be lowered into a mine. Nor would he recognize the Great Britain of his day in such terms as would describe the British Empire as it now is, in the North and the South, and the East and the West, — widening over the traces of the red man in Australia, and the ruins of ancient thrones in the interior of Asia. Nor, were he taken to hear a lecture on geology or chemistry, would he recognize English thought in any thing he would hear. And yet it is still here, the England of his day."

"Where, Mr. May, where?" inquired Percy Coke.

"In the villages, and some of the quieter of the small towns, and in the religion, the habits of thought, and the churches of the Congregationalists. As a small illustration of my meaning, I may say that in this town of Thorpe there are in daily use many words which your English critics, the unwiser of them, deride as American inventions, when heard from across the Atlantic. Certainly I did not expect to find here what I have. From Boston or New York they are distinctly visible, all over England, — the towers of feudalism, and the spires of the Established Church, and the broad roofs of the royal palaces, — and the smoke that goes up from Lancashire and Staffordshire, — and the light that is reflected above London from the midnight sky. But to me it was quite unexpected to find here, amongst feudal institutions, men walking and talking like John Cotton, or like Endicott, — and people living almost as much apart from some English institutions as the Americans themselves."

"Do you think so?" asked Percy Coke, in a tone of doubt.

"While you were a Tory, Mr. Percy, do you remember many times to have met in friendly company with a Nonconformist? Or did you ever know one of your acquaintance have a Dissenter as a friend? I am sure you never did."

"It is matter of astonishment," said the minister, "indeed it is wonderful, in the same town, generation after generation, how distinct they have kept themselves, — the Tories, as they are now called, and the representatives of the Puritans. It is as though, on hearing of the battle of Naseby, or, more truly, of the accession of George the First to the throne, they had laid down their arms, and stood towards one another, ever since, hostile and silent. To a great extent my congregation is composed of families which furnished troopers to Oliver Cromwell two hundred years ago. And at that time the two Royalist leaders in this neighborhood were Wilmot and Burleigh, — and their descendants are still of the same old party."

"Across England," said Martin May, "there may well have been many and many a strong band to hold it together, with such a gulf throughout it as there is between the Church established by law and the Church of the Dissenters. This question of an establisment, — it separates new and old friends more widely than the Atlantic or the Alps, or a great crime. But what amazes me is to see the two great political parties of England playing their artillery at one another across a line of separation occasioned by Puritanism nearly two hundred years ago. While from all around, millions and millions are pressing into the civil war, with passions of their own, and new objects. Still there are heard all about the war-cries of the last century, 'Church and State,' and its opposite, 'Civil and Religious Liberty, all the world over.' But now, instead of five, there are twenty millions of people in this island, — most of them ignorant and hungry. A speech on civil and religious liberty, — what is this to a man who is hungry, and who does not see how or where he is to get a loaf of bread to eat? 'Church and State!' — why should a man shout this, with whom the great object is to find a shop to work at? Twenty millions living on the same little island on which five once did! They have very different troubles, dangers, wants, they twenty, from what the five had!"

"Ah, Mr. May, you have seen further into our difficulties than most of us have ourselves."

"And I am glad that I have seen England as I have. For in twenty or thirty years there will be a change over all the country, greater than that of the whole eighteenth century. Even now, every day, there is change going on fast, from the increasing circulation of newspapers, travel by the railway, and the diffusion of education. Fifty years hence, perhaps, it will be almost incredible, that, by going out of one county into another, you could go from one dialect to another, so distinct as to sound like a different language. And how many will there then be found, of whom it will be probable that neither they nor any one of their forefathers, for hundreds of years, were ever forty, or even twenty, miles away from their native place? And by that time, too, how many of the ancient customs, which are dwindling here now, will be extinct! How many an old superstition, not believed even now, will then be utterly forgotten! And of the different classes toward one another, for better and for worse, how much of the old feeling will be changed! Duke and peasant, language and mental tone, politics and ignorance, — it will all be changed, — England all, from the monarch on the throne to the miner in the pit, in the dark! And by that time your Church will have ceased to be called Presbyterian, perhaps. For even now it is almost the last of its name, I think."

"You are right," said the minister. "For already much that was distinctive of the old English character is ceasing."

"Such things," said Martin May, "especially, as do not get written of. But yet which are very important. And from noticing them I have thought that I have learned much."

"You have done," said the minister, "you have done like John of Salisbury, who said that some things which he had not found in books he had gathered from the daily use and experience of things, as though from a certain history of manners. But on the whole you think of English influences as affecting character ——"

"That they are most diverse; and even of the most opposite natures, — some most genial, and some most unhappy. On one and the same tree, by strange grafting of the same old English stock, are ripened some of the best fruits of freedom, and some of the worst fruits of oppression, and the fruits of hypocrisy, — fair and hateful, and like apples of Sodom."

"You have seen something," said Percy Coke, "of the England of the great deeds, and the great men, and the great past, — perhaps as much as at all survives. For it is not common now, as it was a hundred years ago, that state of mind, of the nature of faith, by which a man was patriotic and devout; and was unenvious in his walk in life, because of his having an eye to the ranks that are higher than the highest human ranks, — the hierarchy of heaven."

"Yes, that is exactly what I do not find, — that old spirit. And, excepting our friend here, I have not met one man of what I may call fearless faith."

"Ah, so it is," answered Percy Coke. "And of those who ought to be strong to speak the words of eternal life, how many there are who are lost in the desert! Water of life, — they need it, they want it, and they desperately dig for it in the sands, along with Jeremy Bentham; or along with the German Hegel, they keep journeying after the mirage; or in despair they return to men who stand by cisterns of their own hewing, — cisterns now broken, and mere remembrancers of water."

"But evermore," said the minister, "the water of everlasting life still keeps springing up from the fountain of eighteen hundred years ago. And always and easily it is to be found by the humble, though certainly only by them, sometimes. And perhaps now, at this time, it is so."

"The end of the year!" said Martin May. "It is so solemn, that it makes many another thing feel so unreal. A strange time this, in which for a man to have to grow earnest in soul; while old opinions are dying out, and old usages are ceasing; and with fierce worldly controversies about him, drawing him into their folly and bitterness."

"But an age not without God," replied Percy Coke, "and so not without newness of life being possible in it. Do not you think so, Mr. Lingard?"

"Yes. But yet I think it must be acknowledged that a man can better be religious in some places and some ages than others, — better here, I think, than in Manchester, and perhaps better here now than twenty years hence, — when it will have become modern bustle, this ancient quiet, which is almost akin to religion. But not that I would speak in this way positively!"

"O, no!" said Percy Coke. "For surely, surely it waits us, — the Church of the Future, with humility for its doorway, and the felt presence of God inside, for a new — or rather a newness of revelation. Though perhaps there will be needed — what will be presented, it is to be hoped — guides by whom men may be brought back from the bewilderments they are lost in, and the idolatries into which their opinions are turning."

"Walk in the Spirit, — is the direction of the Apostle. But that walking is the difficulty. So hard, so very hard, it often is! Though I suppose it is to keep him in a wrestle, and wakeful and strong, that almost every man would seem to have his one folly. Yes, Mr. May, I have. And it is one which perhaps nobody guesses at, though so often it is anguish and tears for me. But what was I saying? O, that always the Spirit does wait on those who are willing to walk by it, and under God and Christ always will."

"Yes, it is so promised," said Martin May, "and I believe that, for comfort and peace at least, myself I have experienced what verifies the promise for me; though no long while ago I was almost in the same case with certain disciples whom Paul found at Ephesus, and who said that they had not so much as heard whether there was any Holy Spirit."

"And," continued the minister, "I am surrounded with things pleasant and vexatious, — things that are duties for me, and some that are pleasures. And amidst these my walk may be in the Spirit; unconsciously so, for the most part, but every now and then sensibly so, by my feeling myself urged to holiness beyond my inclinations."

"It occurs to me just now, how you found me on the river-side, the first time I had any conversation with you. So differently I feel now to what I did then. To me now it would be so dreadful to believe that it was taken, withheld from me, — the Holy Spirit, — and that there was over me no holy guidance ever to be felt on being prayed for, — and within me no source of thought holier than my own corrupt heart."

"But now," continued the minister, "now to him that hath, there is more given. And to him who does walk in the Holy Spirit, all outward things are spiritual helps. And the Spirit of God makes itself felt, not only from within us, but also by things that border our paths, — that meet us on our walks, — that are with us in our homes. And the Holy Spirit, — it influences us not through the Bible only, but also through every good book, — not through Sabbaths only, but through the cold, pure beauty of sunrise, and through the grandeur with which the sun sets, and through the awfulness of the dark. Yes, it influences us, does that Spirit, through the success which rejoices us, and the failure which humbles us, through the public controversies in which we have to share, and through words tenderly and wisely spoken by our friends, and through the ongoing of time, as it enlightens and changes us. And, Mr. Percy, I believe this,—that while we are willing to walk in the Spirit, we are being led into the knowledge of all truth,—all spiritual Christian truth,—into the secrets of the soul's growth in grace, and into the right faith as to the way of God's love and watchfulness for the soul. If any intelligent peasant would walk in the Spirit truly and joyfully, and then say what he saw and felt, I believe there would come from his lips holier words than are preached in this town at least. And the scholar who should walk in the Spirit, and speak his thoughts, would be, if not a prophet, then certainly now the first man after the least of the prophets."

## XLIII.

New Year's morning! O the hopefulness of it for some, and O the thoughtfulness of it for others! New, and new, and new, — so life always is: but it feels so one day in the year beyond all other days, because of people agreeing on that one day to say to one another, " A happy new year to you!"

This morning Martin May left the Dell for Manchester, on his return home. On his way past Thorpe, many persons whom he met, one after another, wished him a happy new year. And it occurred to him, that he had read this very wish on a piece of old Roman pottery from Herculaneum. And while he was thinking of this, he heard the church clock strike nine.

"Nine o'clock of New Year's morning," said he, looking about him. "And this is my last look at Thorpe. How I should like to have just such a glance at my friends, — all of them, — and know just at this hour what they are thinking and doing! It will be five years before I can hope to see any of them again. Five years, — five times a year of days! O, what chances for death! But myself, grown healthy and cheerful and strong, and now on my way home, I ought to be more hopeful. And I will be. And now one farewell look at Thorpe, and then I shall be out of sight of it. But yet I wish I could have just one glance at my acquaintances at this hour."

Nine o'clock, — and Jude Bamforth, eager and successful, had just concluded a good bargain, and was saying to himself exultingly, "Energy, energy, — it is energy that does it.

Nine o'clock, — and Mr. Coke was murmuring his last words, "And so from her to the God that sees her." For he had grown suddenly worse in the middle of the night before, and towards the morning had become delirious.

Nine o'clock, — and, by the death-bed of his uncle, Percy Coke was having his soul drawn into such feelings, and into such an attitude before God, as the Spirit itself bears witness with, — tenderly, persuasively, most solemnly. And there came into his mind, that he had read somewhere, that, for belief in an hereafter, one needs only to have a dead body to look at, and to believe in God. "But," said he to himself, "it is only through Christ, that faith, a sufficing faith, is possible here. It is only a God watching us with the eyes of Jesus Christ, — only God in Christ, — that one can think of, and yearn to, and believe in, here."

Nine o'clock, — and at this hour the minister was meditating on the sermon which he was composing for the first Sunday of the New Year. And because he was aware that the New Year's discourse often gets a little more than the usual attention from a congregation; and because it is a sermon in which the days that are past seem to be speaking to the days that are coming; therefore the minister was intending to have in his sermon, if not something for every body, yet something or other of which almost every one might be expected to feel the force, either on account of some late public event, or on account of the misfortune of some person, which had been much talked of; or on account of some religious difficulty, which one person having felt, it was likely that many others might entertain; or else on account simply of that feeling of human evanescence which rises in the mind of almost every one with ending one year and beginning another.

Before the minister, on the table, lay some papers, on which were written the chief thoughts for what he intended should be his discourse. And as he looked at them he said, " Ah, these may be pearls, perhaps, but they will never be thought so, without being strung on a thread of gold. A golden thread! And then whatever falls from it to each man will quite certainly be reckoned a pearl of wisdom and great price."

Then he read to himself the following, — linking the sentiments together with the thoughts, which he intended to supply, and several times repeating his text, which he fancied was like stringing gold beads with his pearls.

" This life of ours is not pleasure only. It is pain, it is sorrow also, and purposely. It is of such a nature as was meant to make us serious. Though it should make you more serious, yet it is far better that you should feel what life really is. It is infinitely better that you should not think it to be a pageant, while it is reality, and that you should not be feeling it like sport, while it is God's earnest with you.

" There are other troubles than what pitfalls misfortune digs, or what vacancies about us death may make, or what sorrows sin may push us into, or what sufferings mortality may make us feel. There are seasons in which the soul saddens as though of itself. And against these times a right feeling is necessary, as much as it is for those calamitous occasions which grow awful from God's eclipsing the sun from us in the day, or from his making the night be as dreadful to us as though the moon in the sky were turned into blood. The growth of the soul is not all joy; for very often it is sorrow as well. Joy it might be altogether, did the soul open its faculties as easily and orderly as a flower unfolds its leaves. But this it does not do. And so it may happen that a man may be the holier, only to feel life sadden as he advances in it.

"Bitterness, despair, and merely like a curse is the first great trouble that comes to a soul which has not first suffered by sympathy. Old age will wither your soul as well as your body, if as a young man you refuse to grow into the spirit of a suffering world.

"A proud man is a monstrosity when he is thought of. A man prides himself over other men on account of the clothes he wears, the large house he lives in, the way in which he is waited on, and his delicate manner of living; while poor people have coarse clothing, hard fare, and poor lodgings. As though God could not easily have adapted the earth to man in such a way as that the rocks would have housed him like grand palaces, and the trees have maintained him on luscious fruits always ripe, and garments have been yielded, colored like the flowers! A householder, a very comfortable householder, are you? But also you are a dweller in the earth. And it is for you to look out into the world, and to feel some responsibility about it. And really this responsibleness is laid upon you; and if it were not, then it would be good for you to pray for it. When a man becomes independent, and uplifts himself above want, it is well. For he has had the good of it. But to be born above want is a questionable good, unless the man keeps himself in communion with it through his sympathies.

"Let me weep with them that weep, feel for the sufferers about me; let me believe that in part men are afflicted for me to pity them, — that they are lowly for me to enter into their feelings; and then there will be no pride possible in me, nor despair. Let a man live on in the Christian spirit, and he will feel the world grow divine about him. And he will say, 'Always God was here; though I knew it not.'

"Take the Bible and read it. And you will have your soul closer to the soul of Isaiah, than if you held his living hand in your warm pressure.

"Envy nobody; covet nothing worldly; go quietly about your work. And believe that a man may work at an anvil, and be as religious as if it were his office to stand at the altar. Amos, the prophet, said of himself, 'I was no prophet, neither was I a prophet's son; but I was an herdman, and a gatherer of sycamore-fruit; and the Lord took me as I followed the flock, and the Lord said unto me, Go, prophesy unto my people Israel.' But you say that you want to do something signal; that you crave a great opportunity. But more than your hands or your strength, it is your heart that God wants. Be quiet, and do your little duties. Do them for God, be they ever such little things, and then they will become great results. For every godly worker has God a worker together with him.

"O the mysteries of life! It is well worth living the last ten of threescore years and ten, if only to have these mysteries to wonder at, — to wonder at with ever-deepening awe.

"It is come among us, — the New Year! And it is being followed by the months. The months, — one of them is coming wrapped in snow-storms; and another will come crowned with flowers, and will linger long days with her foot on the green turf. The months, — one of them is coming with gain for this man, and loss for that; and another of them, perhaps, is hastening to come and see one of us die. The months, — perhaps one will bring a fair bride for a happy husband; and another will approach, spade in hand, all unexpectedly to dig a grave for some fond father's child. The months, the coming months! O the things they will bring, and the things they will do! Well may we expect them with hope and fear, — with hope that dies away into fear, and with fear that changes and passes into hope. But for us to grow religious we must be mindful of one another, and each sympathize with the other in whatever the months may bring him: and we must have awe towards God for the way in which unceasingly he blends his providence with the round of the year, with sunshine and darkness, birth and death, work and quiet, joy and sorrow, and all human things."

While the minister was intent upon his sermon, Mrs. Satterthwaite approached him with a note. By its look it seemed as though it might have been an invitation to a festive party. But it was really written hastily, to tell of the dying state of Mr. Coke. While laying the note before him, the housekeeper said to the minister, "Please, sir, I wish you a happy new year."

"Thank you, Mrs. Satterthwaite. And in return I wish you a happy new year," said the minister, holding in his hand the unopened note.

"O, dear!" said Mrs. Satterthwaite. "How time does fly! The longest life is but a parcel of moments."

"And so," said the minister, "so, as an old philosopher used to teach, we should live as though our lives would be both long and short."

"It is eleven years to-day, sir, since my poor Thomas was taken with his last illness. But dying is as natural as living. And, as the old saying is, I wept when I was born, and every day shows why."

"And if we will not learn it in humility, we must do so, earlier or later, in confusion. And this is true, as we cannot help feeling. Let us look up on high to God, and then it will trouble us to recollect no tears that we have ever shed, but only perhaps some which we never have wept."

"Ah, yes," said she, drying her eyes, "a good conscience is the best divinity, as the old adage is. And the first time I ever heard it was in a sermon on a New Year's Day, one Sunday, more than forty years ago. Take time while time is, for time will away. Ah, they may well say so! However, we talk and talk, but God does what he pleases. And, as the old proverb says, love may gain all, but time destroys all, and death ends all."

## XLIV.

After five years Martin May returned to Thorpe on a short visit. And as he walked from the Dell up to the town, it seemed to him that he recognized every tree and bush and stone on the way. And as he went along, it felt to him as though he were in a dream; for every object seemed to him both familiar and strange. He met a youth of fifteen, and then an old man with a staff, and then a blushing young lady of twenty. And they all stared at him, and started, and then exclaimed, "What, Mr. May!" "Why, Mr. May!" "Mr. May, I do declare!"

He went straight to the Parsonage. There were the same trees standing; and the gate to it still opened in the same way it used to. It was the same place it used to be; and yet easily he could have believed it not the same. About the house the grounds were very neat; but so they always had been. And to look at, the house was very clean; but then so it always had been. Cheerfulness, — yes, that was the difference which there was about the house. For in the trees the breezes which used to make loneliness audible seemed now to Martin May to soothe the listener with whispers of peace and love.

At the house-door his ring at the bell was answered by a young woman looking full of bloom and happiness. On his asking to see the minister, the young woman said, "He is out; and he will not be home till to-morrow. But, Mr. May, — O, Mr. May, will you not walk in?"

"And so you remember me, do you, Sarah, — Sarah Burtenshaw? But you have returned from London."

"Yes, sir, I am living here now. For when there was a housemaid wanted, Mrs. Satterthwaite had the minister send for me. But do walk in, for my mistress will soon be in. She is only gone out for an afternoon walk with little Richard."

"No, Sarah, no. I will call again to-morrow evening. And give my respects to Mrs. Satterthwaite, will you?"

As he went up the street from the Parsonage he met a lady, who was bending down over a little child that was taking some of its first steps. And he thought certainly it was Miss Barbara Shelmerdine, with some neighbor's child. And soon afterwards he met another lady, who seemed to him like a mother anxiously hastening after her infant. And he looked back, and said to himself, "This road is exactly the same as it was. But even if it were not; and even though they altered ever so often, — the ways of the world, — yet they would not change so often as the feet that walk them."

He sought Percy Coke, and he found him in a field next to his house. He was sitting on a haycock, writing in a note-book with a pencil. And near him, on the hay, sat a little child playing with some wild-flowers.

"How do you do?" When the two friends had both asked and answered one another this common question, they looked at one another for a while in silence. After a few more personal inquiries had been exchanged, Martin May said, "Your book, Percy, your book! You have never let me know how it succeeded."

"It did not succeed at all," said Percy, with a bitter smile.

"O, I do not know that. You have been expecting too much, and too soon. And I have no doubt that great, very great success is a mucn smaller thing than you think."

"Perhaps so, — yes, I dare say."

"You speak up in the world your loudest, hoping to have every body hear you. But then think how many others there are wanting to be heard in the world as well as you, — novelists, historians, politicians, preachers, poets, — a man or more in every town, — a vast multitude of men. Hark how they speak and sing and declaim and demonstrate, read, beseech, shriek, roar, and rave! And among them all, what are you? Your own highest hope, what is it? Is not it that, amid all this noise, these echoes, your own utterance may be something of the nature of a still, small voice? So then for a few years it is enough, success enough, if you can make yourself well heard by me, and a few hundreds of those who are nearest about you."

"A few hundreds! In a whole year there were only thirty-seven copies of the book sold."

"Thirty-seven! No more?"

"Not one more," said Percy, in a tone of some little mortification.

"Not one more, — you are sure of that? Then I am glad, heartily glad. Why, it is ludicrous, absolutely ludicrous. It is a joke. It is Fortune joking with you. And she will own you for her favorite yet, I am sure she will. Twenty years hence, what a tale it will be to tell, — what a joke to laugh at, — what a humble beginning to be proud of! Thirty-seven copies in a year! Thirty-seven copies in twelve months, among thirty millions of people!"

"A volume that had cost me two years of hard work, — nay, thirty years I may say. For of all my life, and all my studies, this book, four years ago, was the whole result."

"Why, it is ludicrous, really ridiculous, that there should have been sold of such a book only thirty-seven copies."

"And perhaps not one of them has been read. For very likely they were all of them bought and opened and pushed aside by people who said that they thought it had been something else."

"Thirty-seven copies! Well, Percy, myself I should rather it had been thirty-seven than three hundred and seventy. For the larger number as a sale might have been reckoned a failure. But the smaller number is not even that. Well, at the beginning I do not know how it should be otherwise with a man like you, — a philosopher of no connections, no friends out of Thorpe, and with scarcely a correspondent. After all, it is not very strange."

"No man is minded, Martin, for the wisdom

which he speaks. A person is listened to, not for what he says, but only for who he is. And who he is does not matter much, so only that he is notorious. I could have a sale for my book now, if I would stand on my head on London Bridge for an hour, or if I would go up on horseback under a balloon, or if the Quarterly Review would either praise me or abuse me, or if I could procure myself to be suspected of treason, or if I would publish some nonsense verses for the nursery."

"It is because of your being so trustworthy that you have succeeded so ill. For an author who is of no sect and no party is a man of no friends, and with the world all round him for his enemy."

"My uncle George was right, altogether right, in what he said as to the difficulty, and almost the impossibility, of my getting a hearing from the public. He was a great man, — a greater man than I at all thought him, while I was a mere scholar. There are sayings of his which sound to me now so wise as well as noble. Even knowing what I know now, I do not think I should have become a merchant, but certainly I should have been more pliant to my uncle's counsel than I was. And I am very sure that, were he living now, he would be able to show me some way in a direction in which I can myself find at present no path. I thought I had only to say to the public, that I wished to speak, and that then I should be heard at once, and thankfully."

"I am not sure but now you think too well of the public, — too highly of its discrimination; or else I should say that in regard to you and it there had been verified the Eastern proverb, that the wise man knows the fools about him, but the fools do not know the wise man."

"But," said Percy, "but after all, I am not sure that the book ought to have succeeded. I wrote it before I was married, as you know. If I had been the advocate of a sect, there would have been more zeal in it; or if I had been the assailant of some established institution, there would have been more heat in it. If I had been a husband, there would have been more tenderness in it; and if I had been a father, there would have been more earnestness in it. It is wanting in heart. I wrote it when I was almost as much disconnected from all institutions and social ties, as if I had been a subject of Caractacus, just come to life again. But I am now very certain that, for a man to be able to speak his best to the men of his time, he must have in him the life-blood of his time. Paul had that; and so had Luther and Latimer; and so have all the best poets had, — Chaucer, Shakspeare, Spenser."

"But from that note-book I suppose you are yet expecting to do something some time, Percy."

"Come here, Louisa, come. Yes, with my child in my eyes, I find I have other thoughts than I have among my books. And sometimes they seem to me worth preserving. And my friend Lingard says that he is sure the hour will come that will call on me for something great, and that I shall say it."

"And he, — how is he?"

"Here he is." And so saying, Percy drew from amongst the hay a book.

"This! This book, do you say, is Lingard's? How strange! How strange that I should never have known it! For all over the States this volume has a most enviable reputation. A man so careless of fame, and apparently so unmindful of every thing but his own immediate duties and the few people nearest him, he was almost the last person from whom I should have expected a book."

"I persuaded his wife, and his wife persuaded him, that it was his duty to write it. And till very recently I do not suppose that five persons out of Thorpe have known of him as the author. Last week there came two gentlemen to see him, with the purpose of offering him a lucrative professorship. And they were not a little surprised at finding him the occupant of a Presbyterian Parsonage. And so, when they found that he was a determined nonconformist, they could do no more than express their great admiration of his genius."

"His wife! Just now you mentioned his wife. But I did not know that he was married."

"Yes, he is. Three years ago he was married to Miss Shelmerdine, a lady who used to come visiting here sometimes, — an excellent woman! A woman of wonderful energy, and almost wonderful goodness! She draws us all into her own ways, and they are always so kind and pleasant. But my Alice, — you must see her. No, you have not: you have never seen her at all, because you have never seen her in a house of her own. There is only one thing on which we do not agree, — she and I; and it is in regard to the minister's wife. For Alice always will say that she is the best of women. Whereas myself I hold that Mrs. Lingard is excellent, is tender-hearted and thoughtful, is very accomplished as a woman, and very affectionate as a wife; and still is only the next woman after the best, the next best after my Alice."

"And on what subject has been your reading, the last year or two."

"Theology, patristical and modern."

"And on that subject you stand how?"

"As I did; and always with my face towards Christ, although one day I stand beside St. Paul, and another day along side of St. James. For I find that I am a man of more moods than one or two; and that for every proper mood Christianity offers a congenial aspect. And so one day I feel like a predestinarian, and another day I feel strong with my free will. And one season I feel that I have to search the Scriptures, and have all human helps about me, in order to arrive at a knowledge of the truth. And another season I feel as though I have only to be still and so have the Holy Spirit flow in upon my soul like wisdom and holiness."

"But consistency ——"

"It is not in the moods of the soul, but in the soul itself. Earnestness in duty, — this is what keeps a soul straight, and on the right path. And on that path a man may walk and rejoice himself with a hymn of Luther's to-day, and with verses of St. Ambrose to-morrow, and at another time with some hymn of Doddridge's."

"I think, Percy, I understand you now."

"I believe with Augustine one day, and with Pelagius another; but when they contradict one another, I disbelieve them both, and I have an ear only to Christ."

"Good!"

"The truth as it is in Jesus is greater than any man can speak logically. Luther utters something of it, and Calvin something, and Zuingle something, and George Fox something, and William Penn something more. But when any two of them contradict one another, I suppose perhaps they are both wrong."

"Good, very good!"

"Winchester and Calvin, John Wesley and John Taylor of the Hebrew Concordance, — all your respective doctrines are true to me, more or less, at one time or another; but when you straiten them into antagonism with one another, then they become false to me."

"But Calvin looking over into the bottomless pit, where souls are in torment for ever; and Winchester turning up to God his ecstatic face, in adoration of the way in eternity by which at last all souls are gathered into the bosom of God, — you cannot believe them both."

"Nor either of them. I will tell you what I mean. In regard to the great future of souls, —

the wretched ones of earth, — I hope with all the hopefulness of Winchester's reasoning, and I fear with all the terribleness of Calvin's statements, — I walk in the sunshine of hope at its brightest, and in the shadows of fears at their darkest. And so my soul in me is kept lively and thoughtful and earnest, and ever at the point of prayer."

"Good!" said Martin May. "That is a good position."

"And," said Percy, "I hold it in regard to several other doctrines, which commonly are regarded as opposites to one another by the disciples respectively of Catholicism and individualism, rationalism and supernaturalism. And this faith of mine — or rather this manner of holding some of the doctrines of Christianity — is in harmony with my belief in the God of the Bible. For I do thoroughly believe in the Scriptural doctrine of God, — the God of a covenant, — a God who loves and hates, — a God who draws nigh a man and withdraws from him, — and hereafter who will punish one and forgive another."

"A belief which is held now only by one man in ten, and by him only in his ignorance. But in your book I think you have shown that really it is a doctrine in which meet and harmonize together revelation at its brightest and reason at its clearest. But, Percy, this little girl of yours,— what a sweet, beautiful child it is."

"Yes, so she is. Here, Louisa, come to me."

"How graceful, how very beautiful! She is like infant poesy."

"To me though she is theology, or at least a help to it. For this little child occasions me fresher and more earnest thoughts in religion than Calvin, or Jeremy Taylor, or any other theologian."

"You deriving to yourself instruction out of the mouth of a babe."

"This child," said Percy, "Louisa looking up to me, and I looking up to God, I have my heart the while fill with other feelings than I have ever known before. And those feelings are more trustworthy, I am sure, than some of the thoughts to which logic conducts me. Yes, and when I perceive through what a cloud of ignorance this child looks up to me, and how she looks up to me aright only on the prompting of her heart, then myself I am conscious that, Christian though I am, yet that I cannot look up to God aright on the showing of my own understanding, but only as it were by looking up along the feelings which rise from within my heart, quickened there by the Holy Spirit."

"Percy, I cannot believe, and I do not believe,

but that you are to do service in the world yet, — good service. But I suppose, even now with your temporary failure, that you are as happy as you can be, or ever will be. O, never fear but you will be a prophet yet, and be stoned. You will be a philosopher, and have readers grow wise on your thoughts, and then deny you. Do not doubt it. You will rise yet in the world, and be a high mark for the calumnies of the malignant. Be sure of that. You will be a wise master-builder in the temple of eternal truth; and you will be paid with something less than the wages of an Irish hodman. Never doubt it. True greatness and its miseries, you will achieve them all. I am sure you will. For it is your destiny to do so, I believe. Though, seriously, I would not have you despair of usefulness for one moment. Here, Louisa, come to me; for we must be rapid in our friendship."

"But not of necessity, I hope, Martin. For you will stay a few weeks with us certainly."

"Two days, Percy, only two days, — to-morrow and Sunday."

## XLV.

On Sunday afternoon Martin May and Percy Coke talked together for half an hour in the grave-yard, before the time of service in the chapel.

"Your uncle was buried here, was he not, Percy? I saw him only twice. And yet there are few recollections of my former visit to England which are equally vivid with my remembrances of your uncle George. A noble man to look at, and I suppose in his day and work a most efficient man!"

"In a tomb underneath this stone he rests from his labors. Yes, here he ceases from his conquests, while easily and triumphantly in Manchester and elsewhere other men are gathering the fruits of them and the rewards. The way of life in this world! At least it is so, and I suppose always must be so, wherever there are ignorance and oppression, and where martyrs have to arise. No, no! Earthly reward, the purest, is not the great, grand end to think of, in the great battle of this world. But this is it, — that when we fall, — as fall we must, only some of us, perhaps, a little later in the fight than others, — that we fall with our faces in the right direction, looking towards God, the great spectator, who never wearies."

"That great spectator, in whose notice of us is all our courage and hope," said Martin May. "Six, eight, ten! I can count here ten persons, who were alive and well five years ago, and are now only names upon gravestones. The earnestness and the labor and the tragedy of life, all narrowed down to a name upon a gravestone! What a humbling sight!"

"But," said Percy, "the secrets that are buried in the grave, sometimes! Think of them, — things which men never knew of, and over which now the grass grows. There must be many a tragedy in life, which is almost only of the thoughts and feelings, and hardly at all of either speech or action. And perhaps some such tragedy may have found its close under this very turf, even though life is so quiet in this town of Thorpe. Of suffering and tenderness and moral struggle in this world, how much more must God see than what we know of! How almost infinitely more! And so we cannot well hope in him too much,—the dear God who watches us."

"Louisa Lawton, the name on that stone, I think," said Martin May, "I think I remember it."

"You may perhaps have heard it before, but I hardly think you can. For the lady came to live here after the death of my uncle, and therefore after you had left Thorpe, and indeed after you had sailed from Liverpool. She was very kind to Alice and myself,—very kind indeed. She was some remote relation of mine, and showed great interest in me. She died, as you see, about two years ago. She was a great loss to Alice and me. We named our little girl after her. She was declining in health when she came here to live. But I never thought otherwise than that she would be spared to us for many years, till one day when she fainted at our house. She was sitting by the window, apparently thinking of something sad. And, to divert her attention, I laid the baby on her lap, and said, 'Louisa Coke, your god-daughter.' But as soon as I had said so, she turned pale and fainted. And after that day she declined very fast, and soon died."

"It must have been in conversation, some time,

that I heard her name, I suppose; for it seems to me that I remember it; and yet I do not recollect ever to have met any lady of her name."

"And now," said Percy, "let us go into the chapel; for see, the people are beginning to come up the street."

Martin May sat in the minister's pew, with Mrs. Lingard. And when he left the chapel, he carried away the conclusion of the sermon, not in his memory only, but also in some hasty notes which he took.

"We walk by the help of the same law of gravitation which the moon moves by. And when it is night, we see our way by the light of other worlds, the hosts of heaven. And our spiritual life is just as wonderful. We are living by mysterious ways, which we hardly think of; and we are aided by remoter helps than we always know. We are devout with the devoutness of ancient Psalms, — with the remorse, the repentance, the prayers, the trust, the hope, — with the heart of an old Hebrew king. And we are believers in the Father through words of eighteen hundred years ago. There is on us an impulse from what Moses was in Egypt, and Leonidas at Thermopylæ. There is with us as our delight a poet whose person has been Stratford dust these two hundred years and more. And every day paradise is sung of, within our hearing, by the sweet voice of one who has himself vanished from sight long ago. There is on our souls, too, a something of beauty that is from ancient Greece, and a something of solemnity from the long, long past. When we speak, the words of our mouth are what they are from what the old Germans were in their forests, and from the manner in which the ancient Romans talked. And our own lives, from day to day, are the wiser and the calmer for the instruction which has come to us from hearts that are now beneath the turf.

"We are strangely related. Our souls are mysteriously connected. We are akin to the past, the ages of the past; and so we may well believe ourselves heirs of the future,— as indeed we are, — heirs to futurity and other worlds."

## XLVI.

Martin May passed some delightful hours at the Parsonage, after the public services of the Sabbath were over. He thought that the minister and his wife in talking together made perfect music, — a duet of sweet sounds, that rose and fell together, always apparently changing into one another, and yet always distinct. In talking with himself, he noticed that the minister quoted the opinions of his wife more than once, but books hardly at all, — neither a Father of the Church, nor a classical author. Indeed, all the day he made but one quotation from any writer, ancient or modern.

After tea Martin May sat with the minister under an apple-tree in the garden, while the females of the family walked about and looked at the flowers. Martin May said, "I hope some day to talk with you on the other side of the Atlantic.

For certainly, sir, some time you will wish to see the beginnings of that great new era which is commencing in the world, — great cities rising in the midst of deserts, and sentiments which are to be great social principles, but which as yet are forming in men's minds almost imperceptibly. You will come and visit the States some time, sir, certainly. And it will be soon, I hope. You do intend coming some time, sir, do not you?"

"Barbara," said the minister, calling to his wife, "Mr. May is proposing to me to make a visit to America. And to do so would not take me more than four months. What do you think of the proposal?"

At first Mrs. Lingard looked almost terrified; but quickly she saw something in her husband's face which reassured her, and she sat down beside him and replied, "Apart from one another for four months! O, no, that we cannot be! Because, Richard, what remains to us of life is not more than enough for all that we have to talk and study and pray and enjoy together. Four months! O, no, we could not be apart while so much time as that went on. And then little Richard, — to think of his growing four months without you to see him! Four months, — O what a gulf of separation! And what danger there might be in it! Ah, no, we will never let it open betwixt us. But we will keep by one another while life lasts, and never be apart for more than a few hours, or at most a few hours' travel."

"Mrs. Satterthwaite," said the minister, "come here. We want you. I wish to speak with you. Mr. May wishes me to return with him to America, and to travel there for a few months. Do you think it would be good for me? Myself I think perhaps it might be. But what do you advise?"

Mrs. Satterthwaite drew her shawl about her, and then made her answer. "The friar preached against stealing, when he had a pudding in his sleeve. For, sir, last Sunday afternoon, was not your text about being keepers at home? It is a good saying, Praise the sea, but keep on land. And besides, the cow does not know the value of her tail till she has lost it; and a man does not know what a loss home is till he is on a journey. And then, too, to travel safely through the world, a man must have a falcon's eye, an ass's ears, a merchant's words, a camel's back, and the mouth of a hog. And I am sure that you are too good a man to be possessed of all those qualifications. However, I have no fear of your going.

For Samson was a strong man, and yet he could not pay money till he had it. And I think, sir, you will hardly go from home without full leave from the mistress. And I am quite sure you would never go away anywhere for a month without permission from little Dick. And he cannot give it, nor indeed speak at all yet."

"There!" said the minister, in a desponding tone. "You hear what they say, — my wife and my counsellor."

"But, Mr. Lingard, what do you say yourself?"

"Do you see that tree against the house? I planted it myself, one day during our honeymoon, did not I, Barbara? Now, Martin May, if I live, I intend to keep within sight of that tree till it is full grown. And by the time it is a large tree I shall be an old man perhaps. And I shall not then be inclined to wander, but, like Peter of Celles, I shall lean my staff against my fig-tree, and have in mind the eternal years."

THE END.

www.ingramcontent.com/pod-product-compliance
Lightning Source LLC
LaVergne TN
LVHW020117110826
845151LV00001B/187

*9781425542672*